Handbook
for the New
Paradigm

Published by
BRIDGER HOUSE PUBLISHERS, INC
P.O. Box 2208, Carson City, NV 89702, 1-800-729-4131

ISBN: 1-893157-04-0

Cover design by The Right Type
Printed in the United States of America
10 9 8 7 6 5 4 3 2 1

*A Personal Message
for You*

I

This is a point in the evolution of the planet that brings to the forefront of each individual's thoughts the question of why me, why now and what is really going on in the reality that is right now in the time we are experiencing. What really is going on behind the scenes we are aware of through the five senses? Why is there this feeling that there is more to the story than just appearances. Who indeed has set this up and is pulling the strings. Is it really just a group of somebodies that is in charge? If this is the case, then is the God thing really a hoax after all? There are those who believe that to be the true essence of the scenario. Fortunately for the good of all, that is not the Truth.

The Truth is that there are multiple levels of activity behind what appears to be a play of incredible magnitude. Who then is writing the lines for the characters and what is the point of the script? Would you be surprised to learn that you are writing the lines and until you can figure out a point to the script, there is none? If that is the case, then which of the individuals on the planet can figure one out? Well, indeed there is a focused group that has decided that they would like to put forth their point in the script. There is just one problem with this: they have decided to put forth a focus within the play that is not in harmony with the Creator of the stage and the theatre that this play is to be performed upon. In fact, the plan this group has in mind has a great surprise at the end for the audience and the actors on the stage. They intend to destroy the audience, the actors, the stage and the theatre.

Since the Creator of this theatre likes this particular theatre and thinks of it as a pet project, this idea doesn't appeal to Him at all. Since He is not in the business of standing in the way of the creative presentations that are produced within its confines, then He is hoping that the audience will decide to make changes of their own. There is a type of presentation that involves participation of the audience other than just sitting and observing. The theatre entrepreneur is wondering whether if the play being presented becomes obnoxious enough to the audience, will they simply walk away and withdraw their attention? This would then allow the cast and its directors to destroy themselves, but then the theatre owner does not want his property destroyed along with them. He is hoping that the audience will come up with some other solution. Perhaps there could be audience participation that would perhaps introduce some new characters that would create lines of script of their own. If a new story line could be introduced with characters that could change the ending, then the performance could be a comedy or a mystery or a love story rather than a tragedy. Maybe audience participation could indeed create a whole new genre of experience. Instead of depicting repetition of experiences already known, could the audience in the intensity of desire change the story line, come up with a creative scenario that would encompass possibilities not yet experienced? Why not? The greater the desire for change, the greater the opportunity for creative new boundary-expanding story themes. Within the spontaneity of group focus, without the academic control of leadership with an intended purpose, conception outside of ordinary themes is not only possible, it is probable.

To what purpose is this discussion being instigated? It is time that you awaken to your responsibility to change the (destination of the) path you are now being pushed to take. It is far past the stage of leading you. It is at the stage of pushing you. It is at the stage where resistance cannot be successful; therefore you are going to have to accomplish this by some other means. A way must be literally created that will bring about a solution. Nothing that you have done before will accomplish a change in this situation.

Those who have brought you to this point know your current human nature so well that every possibility you can think of has been blocked. Every cell of resistance is well known by them and is allowed to exist because it has a purpose in their plan. These will be used as graphic examples of what they will not allow.

Now you must come into the understanding that there is a passage through this experience for mankind, but you must move into a creative stance, not a resistive posture. This is not what is expected of you based on your past modes of experience. I can assure you that your history has been analyzed and studied by minds and computer model to the point that you are known to an extent you cannot even imagine. Every reactive scenario has been dissected to the cellular level and restrictive actions planned for each of them. You are faced with the possibility of your extinction unless you can make a cosmic leap to a level of creative imagination that will completely nullify those plans. Have you not computers of your own? Can you not band into creative discussion groups and ask for entry into the mind of that which created you? "Where two or more of you are gathered together in my Name (within the focused desire for harmonious understanding), there am I also."

Cries and begging to be relieved of the situation by God, or Jesus, Buddha or Mohammed will not do it. You have allowed this evil to descend upon you and so it is you, individually and collectively, that must take it upon yourselves to conceive this solution. A new consciousness change must take place within you. Not all of humanity will choose to participate. There will be some that will hide their heads in blame and grovel in victimhood. So be it. Let them. You have no time to recruit among them, for what of creativity could they offer? This is a clarion call to the consciousness of those with the strength of character to stand up within their own conscious awareness and decide this situation shall not be allowed to continue to its planned completion. Even those who are in the midst of that abominable plan have no idea that the end is indeed to be annihilation. Unfortunately, it is not only planned to be annihilation of the people and the planet, but of realms beyond imagination.

How shall it be done? How can a change come about in the midst of such a lack of understanding of who and what you are? Now, while there is yet time, before the noose tightens, movement about the planet is yet possible. Groups shall come together to stretch their conscious awareness, to invoke the aid of the highest of sources of knowledge to assist them in conceiving a new way of experiencing manifested existence. This must not be copied from any other experience. It must be literally a conceptual leap, not in its entirety, but in invocation of the beginning framework of such an experience. This is not a process that can be spelled out. It is shadowy in the beginning as it is conceived as a possibility, and so it should be. Known boundaries of experience must be transcended. A super-human assignment? Indeed, but not at all impossible. Out of challenge born of desire and necessity comes the conception of that which is different.

Has mankind on this planet been presented with this opportunity before? Indeed, but each time he reverted to known strategies. Now it has been of his creation that this situation exists. It has been his task to make this leap and so he has now made it so that it must be undertaken or face the possibility he may cease to exist. All of this is his own doing. Mankind has no one else to blame, so there must be a 180 degree turn from past refusal to take on the whole project, to taking it on with resolve and dedication.

II

The focus of energy that holds this planet in orbit within this solar system does not require the power of force to do this, but uses an available process that does not require effort. The concept of power has within it the inherent understanding of effort as force. Since thought attracts, you have brought to you the experience of effort, force and power. There are other experiences available that do not use this concept. Rocketry projects are an example. Your resources are used to effort one rocket and its payload into the orbit of this planet and then beyond. Yet you are visited by beings of other planets that enter and leave your planet's gravitational field without this wasteful effort. Does this prove to you that there are other ways to accomplish movement without such wasteful and dangerous methods? The search for answers to this question intrigues the mind. There are many that know these possibilities exist, but are unable to envision the answers without the need of using great effort to resist what they envision ties them to the planet. It is not the gravitational field that ties them here. It is the consciousness. It is the interactivity of thought acting upon thought that eludes them. They know that their thoughts can influence the outcome of an experiment. However the concept that thought once projected can be released to interact within itself and that it can produce an outcome beyond a controlled (desired) outcome is not understood. The need to control, observe and to prove the process prevents them from reaching into new realms of understanding. What is lacking is the ability to trust that the process can only proceed within positive outcomes once it is released to act within and upon itself. Thought released to act upon itself will return in manifestation glorified and in a form more magnificent than the limited focused mind can imagine.

Now the challenge comes to those who desire to be the instruments of changing the negative plans for the destiny of this planet. Can you expand your consciousness to encompass the process that lies just beyond your "grasp"? It will be necessary for you to begin with the basic desire of participating within a new paradigm of experience. However, to leave the known and desire to venture into the unknown requires the courage to release what you feel is the advancement this "civilization" has made from its stone age beginnings into modern technological comfort for many on this planet. Do you know that the word civilization is synonymous with slavery? In order to accomplish this experience, it required giving up the freedom of personal choice in order that group organization might have precedence. Beyond the family, no organization is necessary. Personal responsibility is the keynote of freedom. Cooperation is a natural phenomenon as long as the need to control is absent. The need to control is a learned activity that becomes habitual through the experience of it.

How does one transcend this habitual activity when it is deeply engrained at a planetary level? It has now reached a point that in and of himself, man cannot break this addiction. The adversaries know this well. They are sure that humanity cannot change it. How then will it occur as the primary starting point of the shift to a new paradigm of experience? It can be done by understanding that thought focused and released can indeed act within itself and upon itself. Though it sounds simplistic, and indeed in reality it is simple, it is a powerful tool. In order for this process to work, there are some criteria that must be present. Since it is a process of Divine Order, it must have at its intentional level the desire to coordinate within this perpetual process. The purpose of it must be conceived with the focus of the continued evolvement of those who will benefit from its inception through the outward movement of its spheres of influence. The intent of its purpose is the key to its success of coordination with and within the flow of Divine Order. If this is reduced to a mathematical formula, then its inclusion can not cause a change in any of the Divine formulas that allow the balance of the whole to exist in harmony. Thought thinking within itself would know if it was acceptable or not. That is the reason the opposition cannot take advantage of this process. Purity of intent to harmonize as the motive is a primary prerequisite. The outlining thought must be specific only in the intent of purpose. It must provide direction of purpose allowing the thought thinking process to proceed into Divine Order by releasing it in total trust knowing it is accomplished in what you call etheric levels and will then manifest into this recognizable reality using all the available triggers for appropriate interaction.

How can you know that this actually will accomplish the desired results and is not just another ploy of the opposition to keep you controlled? Have you heard of this on your media reports? Is anyone within the approved world of communication touting this as the thing for you to do? Indeed not! You are programmed to focus your energies into the salvaging of your sexy bodies and in your humanitarian thoughts for the suffering multitudes, as you have another bite of your steak dinner at the restaurant, or at least another convenient hamburger on your way home from your unproductive labors at the computer keyboard. The process through which you receive this information does use the wonders of your computer. It is a demonstration of thought interacting with itself with the addition of focus. It is the focus of your intent that will initiate the process that you desire. Then thought focused through purposeful intent will complete itself in magnificence through the energy of your faith and trust. Firmly holding to the knowing that the etheric form of it was completed in less than the blinking of your eye will allow it to manifest into 3rd dimensional reality. The computer-like processes of the Creation are indeed endowed with quickness. Then again the ball shall be returned to your court for more to be done within your dimension.

III

It is with careful and focused intent that the reality of this earthly experience is being engineered into a pattern of downward movement into the darker and heavier energies that are at the lower end of the scale in which the human body can exist. This makes the contact between the extension (spirit in body) and its Soul (focused source) more difficult. This is not the whole of the intent. This allows for the possibility of the separation of the two energies. Intricate manipulations of this extension energy must be accomplished in order for this to be a possibility. The "capture" of this Soul energy is for the purpose of causing a break in the chain of energies that extend from the matrix of the Soul. It is the belief of those doing this that it will cause a breaking down of the positive energies that comprise the basic building blocks of Creation. In other words, they perceive that causing a break in the return flow of this energy back to its source will cause a disruption in the larger combined pattern of the Galactic matrix. The conception of this group of separatists is that a chain reaction will happen allowing for chaos to such a degree that their focus can reorganize this chaos into their own matrix. This is quite an arrogant and ambitious undertaking. The plan includes many more quite fantastic steps to follow through to its completion. This is not a plan conceived on a moment's notice. It is one that has been put together over eons of time in your counting. However, since their plans are counter to the controlling parameters within which Creation has come into manifested experience, they are unable to take advantage of the processes that also act as fail-safe guards available to the Creation for the purpose of preventing this planned procedure from causing such an event.

Your logical question is how has this rebellion been allowed to continue to this point? The freewill aspect is what has been exploited as the basis for their ability to manipulate humanity to be the vehicle of their power. Yours is the exact state of consciousness to serve their purpose. You are malleable enough to be influenced into desiring change when pressure is applied to the Soul/extension connection, and change is exactly what they want. At each critical juncture in the previous cycles, mankind has been influenced to change what was present rather than to desire an entirely new experience. Within the cycles of energy that maintain manifested Creation at the various dimensions, there are critical points which allow for changing the vibratory parameters of these dimensions. There is within this opportunity ways that they have worked out to create a downward spiral into heavier energy rather than the lifting of vibration as was intended. This can only happen when the mass consciousness of that vibratory level of planetary experience has its focus on experiences at the lowest level of that dimension. As we approach another of these opportunities, you can observe where the mass consciousness is with regard to what you call ethics and character by considering the role models that are currently popular. However, there is a risk for them in their process. There is a point at which their restrictive pressure of controlling the thought processes of the mass consciousness of the planet can backfire and cause exactly the opposite of what they have planned. This will cause them to miss the opportunity of the final dimensional vibratory change needed for completion of their plans.

They have been successful in their use of various techniques enabling them to greatly weaken the Soul/human extension connection. Because of technology and greater understanding of the nature of human experience, techniques have been developed that indicate success in the process of separating extension and Soul. There is considerable over-confidence in the success of the techniques used on individuals as being applicable to large groups of a critical percentage of the mass consciousness. The results of these experimental successes have them quite intoxicated and already savoring the completion of their divergent goals. (However, it is possible to reverse those procedures and reunite the energies into wholeness again, though the complete healing of these beings that have been used as guinea pigs will require much help. The Grace of the Creator shall be showered upon those individuals to assure the Soul matrix is not distorted.)

The implications of this picture are many, but do not despair for in the knowledge of this, you can plainly see that you are not alone in the healing of this situation. It is just that freewill is at the essence of how you got yourselves into this situation and it will be through the use of freewill that you will desire to finally do something drastic enough that will get you through it. You have used change to get you out before and it only altered the situation, it did not resolve it completely. In this case, the scenario is such that it is literally "do or die" to borrow your vernacular. Within the proper choice of focus lies your salvation. Smile, you are on the "winning side".

IV

As each of you comes to understand this is the pivotal time in which to complete a spiritual journey involving multiple trips through the earthly experience, it will become obvious there is not a moment to be wasted in the final hours of this episode. If you are to accomplish this goal and end this chapter of the history of planetary experience, those who have chosen to mock the creator's plan must not write it. This is a time in which you cannot leave this change in the hands of others. It is too great a responsibility to be left to a few. You must make your contribution in order to be assured that it shall be accomplished and that you shall be included in the multitude that make this a reality.

To accomplish this, first you must open your eyes and see what is happening all around you. You must then come to the unpleasant understanding that you have allowed this to occur because overwhelming methodology of deception influenced you and you resisted becoming involved through taking any personal responsibility in changing it. Careful remembering of past intuitive feelings brings you to the truth. You are now and have been aware that something sinister is present. In all honesty you lacked the courage to look at what it might be because of the implications of what it could involve personally. Courage to do this has come through the change of your attitude. The magnitude of the implication of what the planners of this situation are capable of doing to your personal future and that of family and friends has allowed your desire to know to overwhelm your reluctance. This then leads to the necessity of considering this larger implication for the planet and its inhabitants as a whole. This process has brought you to the point of looking directly into the face of truth. Unfortunately, it is not some religious or esoteric concept that is the "truth that will set you free" but what it has been your desire to avoid at all cost. What you must understand is that this truth is about a situation that could end your earthly experience in extremely unpleasant circumstances, and places your eternal existence in jeopardy. The stakes are extremely high and the circumstances are dire indeed!

This is not a time to hide in your usual excuse of "what can one person do?" A large number of "one persons" can accomplish a great deal. Becoming "cannon fodder" is not the solution. It is required that you become a much more subtle influence. Learn one truth now. Subtle energy is powerful and the most powerful energy is subtle. Your bible says, "In the beginning was the word" but words are thoughts spoken out loud, an inaccurate translation. In the beginning was thought! That is the subtle energy that we are asking you to employ. Simply change the focus of your thought. Do not allow yourself to dwell upon the horrors of what is planned for you, but turn your thought to what it is that you would prefer to experience.

You are trained by their methodology to think only about the programmed thoughts of acquiring things, opinions of others, self preservation among thieves and murderers, and escape from self directed thoughts through addiction to TV, movies and Soul jarring music. Last but not least, pursuit of sexual experience, be it in or out of monogamous relationships. There is also the mind-boggling profusion of religious entities to further lead you from the personal quest of understanding the connection to the source of your presence on this planet in the first place. I can assure you that Jesus, Buddha and Mohammed had nothing to do with it. It is not that these beings did not exist, nor that they were not here to attempt to give you guidance in getting through this dilemma, but the messages they brought were distorted long ago. Neither did they come here to "get you out" by your belief in their existence, past or present. They came to teach you that you must get yourself through this by taking personal responsibility and creating through thought a new planetary experience. In this way only, will you be able to move through this painful experience.

You accept this responsibility by making a personal commitment between you and the creative energy that focused you through thought into this existence. You will know how to participate in creating what will replace this living nightmare with a new experience! How? You search for it through your desire to know and to participate in its creation. Then through seemingly miraculous coincidence, how to participate shall become known to you. The critical point of the process is in making the commitment within your own awareness that the most important thing is participating in the creation of an experience that is 180 degrees opposite what is now planned to be your final earthly sojourn.

The evidence of the necessity to do this surrounds you in irrefutable profusion. You need only to open your eyes, consider the changes in your personal freedoms that are happening in quick succession and listen to (hear) the researched evidence in both spoken and written presentations on your radios, internet and in books. Very soon those will no longer be available to you, leaving only word of mouth, so it is imperative that you respond to this information. You are encouraged to react only through your change of attitude and in your commitment to become a part of this subtly powerful movement. There will not be an Armageddon as suggested in their version of your bible. It shall be a replacement of their planned world through shifting the focus of the awareness of the beings on this planet toward that which is desired rather than that which is being forced upon them. It shall be individual inner change that shall conquer the outer forces that plan to control your very essence of self-awareness. Upon the acceptance of this clarion call lies the future of your survival and the experiences that wait for you within eternity.

V

Indeed, this is a glorious day. The rain falls and the air is clean. Rain is falling generously on the planet and Mother Earth begins the washing of herself in earnest. Is it being engineered? It would appear so, but are their contemptuous machines all that powerful? Do not be so sure. Remember that earth is a projection of thought and thought is self-aware and interacts within itself to greater or lesser degrees. Would earth think to a greater or a lesser degree? That is a question to contemplate.

This is a moment in which to be aware of the changing of the guard. It seems that the destiny of the planet has been wrested from the control of its inhabitants, as it would appear the control of the Republic of the U.S.A. has been taken from its people. Movement within the conscious awareness of the inhabitants present has begun. These levels of consciousness are subtle and they are powerful. Notice of this change in consciousness is not at a vibratory level that will alert the negative forces. Its momentum builds within the subtle powerful planes of energy forces that hold this planet in focus. It is thought interacting within itself. It is acting in concert as a changing perception of the mass consciousness that is similar to a natural shedding process. Like the snake, there is an itchiness that is being felt. This process allows for a time of vulnerability and danger from enemies for it is an internal process. The snake indeed goes within an available den because during this internal process it becomes literally blind. All focus is within itself as the process goes through its formation of a new outside experience for it has outgrown its ability to continue as it is. Even the covering of the eyes is changed so that it sees its world anew. Only the death of the snake can prevent this cyclical occurrence, thus it takes great care during this process. This is an apt analogy for our consideration of the progress of mankind through what appears to be a dilemma of great proportion. Just as the fetus grows too large for the womb and must give up its current experience and adventure out into a completely new environment, there are guiding examples throughout nature to suggest this process is a natural phase of manifested life experience.

The separation of man from nature by being herded into metropolitan areas is not an accident. It has been used many times to suppress individual power to control the experience of life. Closely compacted form is more easily pushed to and fro in the effort of moving individuals into experiences that are contrary to their natural desires toward individual responsibility in choosing their life experience. This herding smothers the natural desires and opens the psyche to influence by the confusion that is drawn within the totality of the being. There is a fundamental call within each for balance. The lack of ability to choose experiences freely causes a distortion of energy pattern that brings intuitional discomfort and searching to change that feeling. This need is then led into unending streams of unfulfilling pursuits by those who would change the destiny of this planetary experience. However, there are ingrained patterns of experience that are reminiscent of the skin shedding process that cannot be distorted. The negative forces have their time schedule that must be met. The timing of this process of human "skin changing" is not one that they are privy to know no matter how they analyze and re-analyze the human experience from their perspective. Can you now realize that Thought thinking within itself has created failsafe checks that prevent destruction if at all possible. Again we are faced with that one element that can put on hold even the fail- safe checks and balances. Freewill! Each has personal responsibility for the use of this great gift of the Creator. He has confidence that fragments of Himself may enjoy taking themselves to the edge of extinction for the fun of the adventure. But, just as in your action movies, (a depiction of this underlying adventurous focus) through perfect timing the hero moves through the scenario with hardly a scratch or at least nothing that can not be healed. Sometimes you miss the point of the movies.

You are now at the critical place in the script. It is time to write in the shift of momentum from the bad guys to the hero so that he can experience that unexpected twist of the story line that allows for his harrowing escape leaving the bad guys holding the bag. Let us hope that this is not a Superman or secret agent adventure in which again there is no end to the bad guy and another adventure between them is waiting in the wings. You have already experienced those scripts. Again you have missed the point of the movies. Do you feel that sense of satisfaction of evil vanquished when you leave that genre of movie? That is the point of it. To always leave you with the idea that evil remains no matter what you do. Were not your experiences in Korea, Vietnam and Desert Storm outward depictions of this same frustrating movie? All wars have this same result; it has just not been part of the plan until recently to flaunt it so plainly for you to see. Your ability to discern and react is being tested over and over. Why else would items of what is being "sanctioned" (withheld) from innocent people in Iraq be published in your newspapers. What do these items for personal use of individual innocent people have to do with the prevention of war preparations? These lists were published worldwide. How do you think the people, who uphold their degenerate president who is instigating this, are thought of by the rest of the world? A new movie genre is being released now. In these your people are being held accountable. These depict surges of justifiable retribution (terrorism) and are being planted in the minds of those of other countries. Their ideal of America as the Light of the world is being destroyed by your diplomacy of arrogance toward other countries' right of self-determination. These punishments are seen as appropriate by them for they are unable to resist this injustice on a larger scale. The disturbances used as excuses to interfere within the borders of other countries are made to give the appearance that there is a necessity to intervene for the good of the citizens. These contrived situations are a hoax, created by subversive groups like the CIA. The resultant aftermath of your American intervention is hardly what you are told it is. Guilt at having been used as a tool will not serve to end this charade. Do not waste your time on it. Resolve to be a part of the solution in order that this error in perception may be rectified.

The wakeup call is being sounded and the internal intuitional agitation to shed the skin of this deceptive controlled experience has begun in earnest. The time of choosing to move with the flow of Creation or to remain stuck within the hoax is upon all of humanity. Education, as it is known, is not an advantage. It is within each self-awareness that this process will take place. All are equal in opportunity in this process. Believe that! Purity of response outweighs educational degrees. Those who know the least of what is going on will hear first. You have been educated into the deception that provides the grease upon the wheels of their plans. You have been fooled into supporting them as they carried forth their plans that so far have been focused upon the uneducated and those unable to oppose the power you are giving the manifested evil ones through consent by believing their lies.

VI

In the reality that surrounds your awareness in 3rd dimensional experience, it is easier to allow the seduction of your 5 senses into believing this is all there is to the duration of your stay within your body. Indeed this has been further enhanced by the introduction of the visual aids of photos, movies, TV and computers. To this add telegraph, telephone, satellites plus music and sporting events all beginning in childhood at the earliest possible moment. Where is there, within this onslaught of mind boggling confusion of distractions, time or desire to contemplate within silence anything but a replay of these experiences? The conscious awareness tries to clear out the clutter of this overload so that contact can be made with an inner awareness and contemplation can begin of how and why you are within this experience. This is a process that goes on quite naturally, except when the conscious half of this combination is overloaded with stimuli. It should be immediately apparent to the reader that this is the case in modern North American/European parts of the world. Furthermore, it is spreading to the more affluent elements around the planet. Once exposed to this mind stifling process, it appears to be relaxing. It is not relaxing, it is mind suppressing! The creative, self-contemplating portions of the awareness are being shut down. The more the experience is repeated, the more of an addiction is acquired. Instead of enjoying mentally stimulating experiences, these are experienced as disquieting and downright irritating. Thus you see the joggers with their wired up ears listening rather than contemplating their own thoughts. Somehow, they must stay connected to their addiction to distraction. If not radios or tapes, then it is car phones to stay connected so one can pontificate with their "friends".

Can you, reading this, separate yourself from the distraction process to contemplate and absorb descriptions of the wondrous fantasyland existence you are experiencing? Where is what you call reality within a world that is mostly pretend? When you look in truth at the information you trade daily through your computer connections, how much of it is indeed concrete manifested reality? Is the money transferred from one account to another actually stacks of bills? Do that many stacks of denominations of money actually exist? Where are there bank safes to house trillions of dollars? Wake up! You are dreaming! Ah, but if you wake up you will have to face the solid reality that you have been used, and that is too frightening to contemplate! How long do you think this dream bubble can go on expanding before it breaks of its own thinness or perhaps because there are ones that will enjoy pricking the bubble? Would it not be best to wake up early and begin to dream a new ending to the nightmare in disguise that you are now experiencing? Can you do that? Of course you can. It is your dream. That you have been programmed to dream a particular scenario can only continue as long as you allow it. There is something called lucid dreaming in which you awaken to an awareness that you are dreaming, then you can stop at that degree of consciousness, observe yourself dreaming and change the scenario of the dream. If you are being chased, create a safe hiding place, have the pursuer fall into a hole, or a train come between you, and you escape.

You have been lulled into a dream state by the distraction of your conscious awareness in order to separate you from your self-aware state (which is the state in which you can observe your dream process). You can correlate this into an awareness that will allow you to reclaim the severed connection to both parts of your total awareness. In truth, your intuitive awareness is beginning now to become awake to the truth of this information. Do you know that you have the power within yourself to encourage this feeling and come out of the unnatural state of distraction into full awareness? This waking process can allow you to avoid the fear and panic that you think facing it might bring, and instead give you an ability to discover yourself as a focus of energetic and creative expression. It will not awaken the "brute caveman" persona you might expect. Instead a contemplative ability to focus upon solutions will come forth that will replace what was formerly sensed as an undefeatable force and an unsolvable situation. This force was smothering you in a deepening dream reality that you will discover does not even exist. It may appear so to the five senses, but you perceive that beyond those lies a potential that supersedes what you have known before. It is the same potential that pulls entrepreneurs into successful businesses and explorers toward unknown places. It has an enticing intuitional call that pulls them from the known, to desire an experience that is unknown and holds such a vibration of potential of success that it cannot be resisted. Many hear the call, but few choose to answer it. That does not mean that it does not exist. The success stories are proof enough of its existence.

It is hoped that this is information for you to contemplate apart from your normal mesmerizing existence. Is there something beyond this enticingly humdrum existence that could be even more rewarding? Indeed there is!

VII

"Around the World in 80 Days" was a marvelously funny satire on good and evil in competition. Don't we wish that the same scenario in one's own reality could be as carefree and funny with all the pratfalls and hair-raising potentially dangerous scenes? You can rest assured that the observers of the play upon the stage of planet Earth are not laughing at the similar scenes as they pass through your manifested reality. Instead they watch through detached wisdom knowing that the ending will be a positive one, but with concern for how many awareness points shall move with the ascending transformation process and how many will be left behind to be shepherded through the process of another opportunity. It shall be a great relief to these when the Earth experience in this particular point of focus will have been completed. Just how it shall all come together has become of major interest, for indeed you have created your own grand and spectacular stage play. The story line is quite unique, something like "The Perils of Pauline of the Galaxy."

It is noted that the terms of Universe and Galaxy are tossed about with abandon and you find yourself puzzled in attempting to correlate these into a meaningful 3rd dimensional understanding. In truth this is not quite possible, but we shall make an attempt at doing so. Galaxy refers to the flow of manifested reality around a center of focus. Universe refers to the focused intent of coagulation of energy that in your terminology lies behind and supports this manifested reality. There are Universal Laws that allow for the creation and maintenance of this Galaxy. Since you are part of this Galaxy (you have named Milky Way), then if you are to experience in harmony within it, you must live within these laws. In this case, you are like children playing "pin the tail on the donkey," for these laws have been withheld from you and you are left to discover them by trial and error. Right now, you are far into the error process. Is this how it has been ordained for you to learn them? INDEED NOT! The blindfold has been deliberately placed upon you and you have been fooled into thinking that you have no right to remove it. The blindfold is the game of deception in which you are enticed to look where the magician deliberately presents action for you to watch while he supports it with motions you do not perceive. Your attention is focused on what you think is the only action.

Fortunately not all the audience is fooled. They watch you and wonder why you do not see the process the magician uses. The fact is they wonder why you are now at a stage where you only perceive his spotlighted action and do not even see the magician. You are so mesmerized that indeed the supporting motions to the actions are no longer even hidden. They proceed all around him on the stage and still you see none of them. How is this possible? By hypnotizing the conscious mind!

Luckily there is another part of the mind that is beyond this conscious thinking. Your psychologists call it your subconscious mind. They have painted it as holding your perception of Life hostage because it is full of dark, horrible experiences perpetrated on you by well meaning but abusive parents. As a result you fear it and block it from participating in your experience of Life. Why is the word Life capitalized? Because that is the purpose of your experience on this planet! You are alive, that is aware of experiencing this Life energy moving through you and played out on the screen of your observing ego mind. Ah, the ego, the devil of your existence, or so you have been led to believe. Anyone acting in a pushy manner is being egotistical. His ego has him by the necktie and is causing him to misbehave according to the imposed social norms. He is controlled by his evil sub-conscious acting out through his ego and he must be brought down a peg and that awful ego humbled into compliance. The successful businessman is successful because his inflated ego runs amuck over others and snatches success from the hands of the deserving underlings, etc., etc. Need I go on painting this picture of sleight of mind?

What then is the true picture? If there is no ego, there will be no awareness of the manifested experience! The ego is your tape recorder. It is the observer of your thoughts, wants, needs and desires. It takes these thoughts in a type of robotic focused format, and this allows them to manifest into circumstances and situations that create your experience. It literally filters your thoughts, feelings and desires and causes them to coalesce into manifested experience. It is a process, not an entity. It is a process over which you have complete control, if you can take charge of thoughts, feelings and desires and actively direct them toward what you want to experience. These thoughts must be relatively depictive. For example, if you simply focus on change then expect chaos within your life for that will be the change you create until you decide upon some more precise idea of what you want in your experience. The process of how this works involves a Universal Law called Attraction. Once an idea is formed with the positive understanding that it is possible, then the ego holds this picture and completes the process through positive/negative polarity energy.

Through the action of the Law of Attraction and the malleable nature of the potential of an idea actually coming into your experience, it does. Since instant manifestation of ideas on this planet at the moment is very difficult, the ego incorporates the process within your supporting idea of time. If you are unable to remain focused on your desire of a certain experience, then often times you deny yourself that desired experience. There is a comment in your Bible regarding "praying amiss". Since that which you refer to as God is creative in nature, whenever you are focusing your desire in a sincere manner for an experience, then you are in "constant prayer" for you are within this creative, expansive expression that originates within the Source of your existence.

But, what if you are asking for something that would cause problems for someone else? The law works! But, there is an effect for that which you have caused. As noted above you are using the Universal Law of Attraction and its process involves like energy attracting more like energy. If you cause a problem for someone else as a purposeful use of this Law, then what you create for someone else, you also will experience. It is like two sides of the same coin. One is presented to the other person and one is presented to you. If you are serious in attempting to understand this Law, then if you dare, look at the events that you have already experienced and you will see that this has been the case many times. When you have wished a blessing for someone else, you also experienced one, not in exactly the same way, but in something of meaning that came within your Life. Consider also difficulties. I believe there is a reference in the Bible that instructs you to "put a guard on your mouth for the words (including thoughts) that come forth do not return to you empty."

In utilizing this understanding, you must hold the desire steadily within your consciousness. If you err in desire by wishing to create a problem in the life of another you have time early in the process in which to reconsider and to withdraw the focus of that intent. Then it will not manifest for them to experience. Emotion, strong feelings, can increase the potential of manifestation and hurry the process, whether it is for your own "good" experience or for another one. The opposite is also true.

It is time for the entertainment portion of this purposefully written portion of the play, and the distraction of your attention from your purpose for being within this experience on planet Earth to end. Now you must decide whether to take back your power, remove the blindfold of your own volition or wait until it's removed for you. The picture will be even more shocking if you wait, for you will be totally unprepared for the scene planned for you to view. There is little time remaining for you to make your decision. The glitzy world you are living within is an illusion. Behind its facade is another one that plays out a game of power that requires your total cooperation and the giving over of your creative power willingly by overwhelming your sense of possessing any personal power whatever. Example: "But, what can one person do?" Sound familiar? Answer: "More than you can possibly imagine, but first you must realize that you have the power!"

VIII

When the conditions of deterioration surround you, how can I comment that this is a glorious day? Indeed, it is, for those conditions are drawing to a close. The ending may contain many surprises. Your Armageddon will arrive, but it shall not be in a format that you have been told to expect. The forces of Light and darkness shall not parry and thrust in a format of war, but nonetheless the situation will have moments of what might be called confrontation but it will not be in a 3rd dimensional battle of armaments. This should be comforting for the power of even those 3rd dimensional devices can destroy the planet.

If indeed the Creator is a focus of Love, then methods of destruction would not be possible. These are only possible within the distorted use of negative polarity energy. Within the two foci of positive/negative energy lies the center point of harmony. This is the goal of all manifested energy, to exist within this harmonious point. However, it has one disadvantage in that the still point existence would allow for no movement at all, thus it can be maintained for only a relatively short period. As a result there is constant movement away from and returning to this ideal.

Within the totality of the Galaxy, there is a balance between portions of it moving away and toward this still point. This is seen in the movement of planets and what you perceive as the Mazaroth or Zodiac as they move in cycles around the center point of the Galaxy. Within these revolving movements are many smaller cycles that you cannot observe. When a distortion occurs within one of the smaller cycles it is allowed up to a certain point. When it reaches a point at which this distortion begins to affect larger cycles, then attention is focused to correct this distortion. This attention is now on planet Earth. Destruction would indeed affect other cycles. One planet in your solar system was destroyed. Balance was maintained with great difficulty, but the loss of another planet would cause chaos that would be far reaching indeed. For this reason a great deal of attention is now being paid to your situation.

If it were not for the limiting factor of the freewill of the inhabitants, balance could have been obtained long before this point. This emphasizes the importance of obtaining consent through deception of the inhabitants for the introduction of atomic destruction devices. Plans are afoot to create the very chaos that planetary destruction would bring. The stakes are very high indeed in this game of control. The plan behind this destruction is ambitious beyond your imagination. It involves the creation of a negative polarity universe/galaxy. To the perpetrators of this situation, you are not even small fry in the game. This is confrontational at the level of the Creator of this Universe/Galaxy. Have we made this up? Indeed we wish we could tell you that, but it is the usurping of your ability to make freewill decisions as to whether to cooperate or not that is the small key to the success of their plan. This will allow you to understand the multiple levels of control that have been used and why your complete control (which of course is impossible) has been used as the manipulation behind your deception. Indeed, there are many levels of control of the people on your planet. Those who think they are in control and planning this scenario are just as controlled as their plan for you. As this plays out, there are elements within this situation that are going to be more surprised than your general populace. However, perhaps that surprise will be at a higher level than even that plan includes.

What must be remembered in the greater perception of this is that all that exists, and that does mean ALL, does so out of the potentiality that underlays manifested Creation. In following the layers of energy that coagulate into manifested realities in reverse order, the building blocks become finer and finer in vibrational quality until it reaches beyond what the Cabala calls Ain Soph or pure potentiality. In order to cause an entire Galaxy to change polarities it would be necessary to return to this point to cause such an event to happen. Needless to say, this is an extremely simplistic explanation, but should give you an understanding of the audacity of the idea and the relative chances for its success. However, the attempt to do this by working backwards through existing Creation to accomplish this goal holds within it the possibility of a pattern of resulting chaos of no small proportion.

Now to come upon the realization that your conscious consent had to be obtained in order to accomplish this should give you cause to take notice of your responsibility in all of this. Unless you wake up and change the path down which you are moving, there is great responsibility to be faced. Granted you have been lulled into a zombie-like existence, but that has been your choice through lack of personal responsibility toward yourselves and your fellow man. At the end of this sojourn into Life experience, you stand and recount your experience in the light of full understanding and it is you who judge your own actions. No one judges you. You are then aware of what might have been had you lived your experience through extending the Love that created you rather than in pursuit of distractions that gave you no real satisfaction.

What now do you do at this pivotal point in your time? In the knowledge of this picture, which you are hardly able to acknowledge may even be a possibility, what can you do? First you must contemplate this understanding and come to face it within your own conscious thinking process. You must consider it as possibly being true. Then you must admit to your unknowing complicity in the treatment of your fellow human beings on this planet. You must move through your regrets for having been unaware through a process of denial, for the existence of these situations was plainly presented to you by the magician. This use of your consent was by real conspirators with very large agendas to put into place. You cannot linger in the destructive guilt process. You must resolve to come into your personal responsibility to cause this situation to change from its intended path. You are expected to stop being a victim and certainly not to become a martyr for there is no place to begin to resist this onslaught. You must vow and commit to become part of the solution. Then, despite the continued push of deceptive encroachment into your awareness, you must begin to discern what is truth. You must hold to your resolve to move through this to a new and greater understanding. When this becomes your greatest personal Truth, then you will find opportunities to become part of a different movement employing methods that will not constitute physical resistance, but will use an entirely new approach. There is no other way open, for resistance on a physical level would be immediately snuffed out. Your constitution is no longer an effective shield and will be dissolved. But, that matters not. It is in assuming personal responsibility that when one accepts the challenge and does not fade in fear, others also shall come forth in like awareness and consciousness. Together this spreading group awareness shall provide the pivotal point that will bring an end to this situation. The resolve to be part of the solution from the depths of personal consciousness is the key that will open the lock, end the imprisonment of humanity and bring true freedom to the inhabitants of this planet. Many are called, but few choose to respond. Where do you stand at this pivotal point? You must ask yourself and you must answer yourself!

The question of "who?" is the focusing energy of the "messages" is a difficult one to answer tactfully and yet completely. "Isness" is the focus to be sought by each individual awareness. As each expands within the process of self-identification so does the ability to allow the flow of "Isness" to move through their experience. Each will attract into their awareness knowledge to live into wisdom. The vibratory rate of the planetary environment and of the members of humanity on earth is low enough that this ability is currently virtually inaccessible. To assist willing members of mankind to access the necessary information to provide a way to transcend this current aberrant state, various volunteer awareness points within higher vibrational frequencies have acted as booster stations to focus this information through those willing to participate on the earth plane. Knowing the custom of earth's inhabitants requiring the "personify to identify" mode, names from the exotic to the ridiculous have been given as sources of this information. The information included exercises in discernment: most participants failed the discernment tests. Much was filled with profound truth, but much of it was drained of energy by the continual parade of victims wanting their personal problems solved for them. The information became distorted as the foci were withdrawn and the volunteers winged it (faked it) on their own for their sincerity was lost in the notoriety and greed that resulted.

In view of this history, it was the mutual agreement between the parties involved in the dictation/translation/transcription process for these messages that the identities of the foci involved would remain undisclosed and there would be no monetary rewards whatsoever involved. Further, there would be no personal information disseminated for any one individual's benefit. The totality of the foci involved is for the benefit of the planet and its inhabitants, period! The truth of the messages is to be discerned and used for the benefit of humanity first and then gleaned by the individual to apply personally as part of the wholeness to which it is focused without the necessity of personal names to identify truth. If that is not understood, then the messages need to be read again to transcend this need into commitment to the holographic intention of the information they contain.

It is hoped that the succinctness of this message is accepted in the tone of importance in which it is intended. The window of opportunity to accomplish the necessary monumental consciousness transition is small compared to the obstacles within the human belief systems that must be literally dissolved so that the whole may be transformed.

It is sincerely hoped that the truth contained will be a sword that cuts through the armor of deception and lays open the hearts and minds of the necessary quotient for success.

No. 1

It is time now for the people on earth to begin preparing for the planned changes in earnest. Many prophecies have been given to you, so many as to be confusing. This has made it possible for most to do nothing because how could they prepare for so many different possibilities? It is imperative to begin with the most basic steps. Consider what are the most basic needs of man in the particular climatic region that you live in? Where you are with winter coming on it would be food, warm shelter and water? If warmth would be critical, it should be addressed.

Let us take a hypothetical example of an earth change "disaster." Suppose there was an especially severe winter storm in your area. This would be a storm that involved high winds, extreme cold and quantities of blowing and drifting snow. The electrical power would of course be cut off. Even if gas was available, it would be unavailable to you unless there was a gas powered fireplace. Without electricity, you could not cook on your electric stove. There would be no electric lights. The streets would be impassable and probably telephone lines would be out, so you could contact no one. What would be your plan? Have you even thought one possibility through to this extent? I suggest that you have at least basic emergency supplies available at home or perhaps in your auto as you are seldom anywhere without it being close by. A camp stove with fuel, some canned or dehydrated food, sleeping bag and most important of all — *water!* Be sure all is in working order, test everything to be sure you know how to use it, see that all parts are there. Know what it is that you would do.

Watch your weather forecasts and be aware that any potential storm can be strengthened and steered. Instruments are in place and in use with the sophistication to do this. (HAARP) Inasmuch as we cannot interfere, we cannot protect you from this possibility. Of course this discussion has centered on only one of many possibilities. You may expect these to be happening around the planet as the equipment is tested in order to understand its capabilities before coming up with a planned sequence of scenarios to help them achieve their goals. Check your food supplies. Long keeping winter vegetables are a wise investment and do cook them to learn how, for most of you have fallen into the prepared food trap. Available lake or river water could be frozen and is seldom pure enough to drink. Water storage is wise and even that will not stay pure without special care. A camping purifier pump is available with extra filters. Consider adding a first aid kit, change of clothing. etc. I strongly suggest that you take stock, make a plan and actually put together a workable short term emergency kit and have it in place. Once that is completed then add long term necessities on a regular basis. Once this is accomplished, you can then turn your attention to the business at hand.

There was an old typing class exercise. "Now is the time for all good men to come to the aid of your country." It would seem to me that this is most appropriate now. But in coming to the aid of the country, one must put him/herself in a position of confidence so that in a crisis attention can be turned outward to those in need rather than scrambling to meet one's own personal needs.

In closing our first session, I would remind you that the days of greater chaos are drawing closer in an ascending quickness. Let us continue these sessions so that our clarity may increase and our messages may become truly a guiding light in the darkening of the days ahead. Sometimes it is necessary for darkness to descend before people can become aware of a light that has been shining all along. Thus shall the coming together of the true family of Light Bearers serve to vanquish the deeds of those with dark intentions. Always remember things work together to bring forth that which was planned long ago, for God's plans cannot be thwarted. The duration and complexity of events can be altered if there is a faltering of faith and action on the part of those that have been placed in stations of service. None are placed who do not have the ability to accomplish their missions. Some will falter and perhaps even fail. That, of course, is a possibility, but back-ups are in place and things will move forward in Divine Order. If you trust the knowledge that there is indeed an overall plan, a larger picture, and that it will succeed, then your own courage and faith will be less likely to falter. TRUST THE PLAN AND PAY NO ATTENTION TO THE DAY-TO-DAY DETAILS. THIS KNOWINGNESS WILL BE YOUR ROCK ON WHICH TO LEAN. YOUR TOUCHSTONE OF FAITH.

No. 2

Let us begin on this new day in quest of a new day. The people of your planet sink further into the morass of depression and suppression. There is nothing but doom and gloom reported all around them and for lack of a vision of Light, all appears to be fading into darkness. The focus of attention on the devils of the dark doings does not resolve the issue. In order for Light to triumph over darkness there must be a vision of the Light that translates into a recognizable reality. Let us use the birth of the United States as an example. Though we cannot cover the details, we can look at the process, as it is known. There were those who came together to envision something that was different than what was currently being experienced by the planetary inhabitants. No one person brought forth the vision, it was a composite of the inspirations that were but pieces of the whole.

This process must be repeated again. There are those who believe that you should return to what you have had before. Let us say that even that would not resolve the issues at hand. The "founding fathers" did not have instant communication, the Internet, exotic surveillance methods, under and above the sea devices as well as horrendous weapons of destruction with which to deal. You have allowed these to be created and though you long to return to a simpler time, you will either tame these or they will destroy you. You must look past the need to merely survive the methods of trickery designed to annihilate you and dream what you would have instead of the chaos of darkness. It is as simple as that, for as long as you choose to merely withstand and only survive the onslaughts of the oppressors, you are sinking deeper into the morass. You will only rise to the top with a new vision. We cannot give you that vision. The book of Spiritual Laws provides some guidelines, however the vision must be simple to be powerful. It must be visual in its simplicity so that the people now surrounded in darkness can literally be struck with its beauty and feel called to its simplicity and clarity.

How do you do this? A small group cannot do it alone. A nucleus must come together and as they begin the process others of vision will be drawn to it, in fact literally sent. The time for beginning this project is not at a convenient time later, but now. There is no time to be wasted if you are to accomplish this. To tarry will only make it more difficult and bring more suffering to the already oppressed. The window will close in literally weeks if it is not begun. I know you are caught up in the process of illuminating the details of the chaos, but what has that done to stop it? Can you actually see anything happening to change the speed of the decline? Then you must change your perspective. Look in the opposite direction. Are you part of the problem by observing it or can you become part of the solution by looking for the building blocks of what you want instead?

Begin in your meditations to ask who would serve well in this project. This is not an esoteric process for people who are looking to give lip service and stand on the sidelines and observe. This is for visionary realists that may never actually observe the extent of the work they do now until the very end. These people will be able to look beyond the chaos and recognize the opportunity. I suppose you might say these are people with one foot in each world, who can look into both without losing their balance. Once you start looking for them you will find them coming into your experience in ways that may seem too unusual to be accidental. Meet in 3s, 7s and 12s. This is the most important step to be taken now. Know that all help possible will be given on request. Many ideas will float through, but those of value will take root and the dream will become real, but first it must be conceived before it can be born. You need not feel total responsibility for any phase, only for the initial promotion of the idea.

The hour is desperate and the plans of God hinge upon the people of service. The awareness of the need for change is well established in the consciousness of many; now the vision must be planted, that it may sprout and come to fruition. May your day be blessed with the Love that is yours, for you are Love in manifestation. It is your job and your privilege to focus it that God may stand forth in Freedom and Truth in the experience of his beloved children.

No. 3

It is our hope that the process being initiated will bring together a nucleus of such compatibility as to be a cohesive cell, which shall mimic the bodily process of cell division. Within such a process, the spread would be quite amazing. Remember a babe begins with the combining of just 2 cells and becomes a being of trillions in a matter of 9 months. By the Law of Attraction, a Universal Law, this is entirely possible. Of course the nature of the babe is determined by the birthing combination. It is the characteristics of these that shall have a profound effect upon the end product. Do not worry. Ones that should not be included won't be, but there are many that are appropriate. Just relax and allow the process to flow, which doesn't mean that this phase is yet complete. Indeed it is just beginning. Just setting minds to considering such a possibility will not bring commitment. You are most important in the birthing. It is those with receptive hearts that are willing to begin the processes that are important. The character, openness to act beyond the confines of the present moment, the ability to make and keep commitments, the love of fellow man beyond themselves, the desire to rise above the trees to see the forest: these are the critical components for these parents. Through this process the awakening of man once again into the "family of man" is possible. The ability of man to transcend the present self-made dilemma into a new concept of experience will bring about a change not only individually but to all, and a ripple effect will be felt throughout the Universe/Cosmos. I know that this seems like a big assignment to begin from just 2, but each new child is also a miracle. Its beginning is hardly auspicious. Just a mass of dividing cells with no apparent organization into a miniature babe. But, at a miraculous moment, the appearance in miniature is there. Inspiration shall begin the change within the focused group consciousness.

The project assignment is that each new cell continues to divide. How exactly is this going to work? The first meets with two. Then each meets again with two others, then each again meets again with two others until there are 7. (3 plus 2 equals 5 plus 2 equals 7.) Then that group meets and the 4 additions split and create their own 7. Now the originals at that point can again begin a new cycle or drop out. The more times each individual repeats the process, the more the growth cycle accelerates. Can you see how the original organization can grow quickly without bringing great danger to the project or to individuals? At this point it is only the dream that is being promulgated. Then the babe takes shape at the critical point of greater group awareness, then the plan changes and the organs, so to speak begin to take shape for the different functions necessary for the creation of the dream. Since the focus is on the creation of a new experience, armaments are not a part of the picture and less danger is present. The focus is not resistance because forward movement into change is not factored into the detection process as presently set up by the oppressors.

I shall leave you to consider what you have been told this far.

No. 4

Fear in the heart puts a damper on the appreciation of the wonderful gift of life. It also hardens the belief of separation and causes those wrapped up in it to become deadened and wooden in their ability to perceive changes going on around them. It is like a cloak being wrapped around the awareness. In this way the darkness wraps its insidious plans of subjugation and annihilation around your fellow earth beings.

Now begins in earnest the movement of the Light to bring an end to this situation. As with all things it begins with the process of thought and desire to bring an end to it. In this case, the subtle, modest beginning will go unnoticed. The opposing forces are planting their seeds of perceived invincibility everywhere. If this were real, they would not need to do so at the level of a psychological campaign. Remember that humanity now numbers in the billions. That is an overwhelming number in itself. These are souls that are volunteering to be here for the benefit of this planet and these beings have incarnated here for the purpose of experiencing the next rising or at the least to assure its success. They shall not go unrewarded.

Remember that this is a play. It is difficult to get this understanding across, but in a play, all you have to do is to change the lines to change the scope of the play. Well, you are a fragment of the whole of Creation and can begin changing the lines of the play. Is this an over simplification of this situation? It would appear so from your prospective, but indeed it is as simple as that. This project involves the formation of the group entity that can change the lines, or add a new character, however you want to visualize the process. Remember a visualization involves pictures. The words that you use in your contacts with those who might become the critical parents of this entity will respond to that which stirs their imagination and their emotions. Learn from your successful political elections, which appeal to emotion before logic. What works for this instrument of the opposition with the people can work for you also. The logical approach brings lots of rhetoric, but it is that which brings visualization and emotion that incites action. What is wanted here is action, not reaction. Resorting to the use of arms against the plan for overwhelming mankind is doomed from the start. Yet the keeping of their guns by the citizens of this country, means that their freedom is not yet gone. When those are taken, then you will see a real overwhelming realization among your people of the gravity of what surrounds them. Thus the timing is again stressed. We do not mean to belabor this, but there are windows of opportunity that must be used for our advantage for these offer the greater chance of success with the least amount of suffering for the greatest number.

Insofar as grieving in regard to those that are suffering, let me assure you that the number of souls incarnating on this planet increases the difficulty of *their* plans. (Note that I avoid using certain names, and you would be wise to do that also after all within your circle the exact identity of these forces can be assumed as known.) Their role is well known to them before they incarnate. They don't remember it now of course, but they come to assure the success of the process of our mission. Does that assure you of the importance of the earth in the total scheme of the grand picture? I would think so.

In the initial meetings of the small groups, no one visualization is likely to appeal to all, so one suggestion shall be given as guidance. "Ask and it shall be given." A composite will emerge that will provide the appeal when participation reaches a critical stage. This diversity will aid in the masking of the process. You are well connected, so do not be concerned about this aspect. Use the visualization of dominos standing on end and arranged in a pattern so that when one is made to fall, all follow in rapid progression. It has great application to our meaning and brings an identifying tie to their planned process.

No. 5

It is resistance to recognizing the situation and more resistance to being responsible for the changing of it, as well as the induced feeling of overwhelm that blocks the participation of the majority. The willingness to be responsible for personal conduct and to change the focus of perception is buried within the busy (frantic) schedules of daily existence. Individuals find solace in their excuses for not confronting the growing signs of coming oppression. Breaking down this line of resistance and drawing as many of these into the new planned pattern of Life remains the goal. Those of the dark plan have set their focus to overwhelm any human beings with plans to resist and have preconceived plans ready to move toward the crushing of resistance. However there are none for the coming of a new vision. This leaves that opening available to us, in fact, the ideal opening. Our plan is not to fix the old, but to create the new.

(There will always be the repetition of certain ingrained habitual thoughts, hopefully not to the point of nausea.) The skill of speaking, indeed even thinking, discretely on the subject of those with plans contrary to the will of Creation will aid in helping to bring that style of referring to them into usage. The more variety in this application of presenting the subject being discussed the better. It is easy for focused individuals to "get right to the point" but this will not serve in the long run.

It might be appropriate to point out that a linear progression within the scope of this project will not always be apparent. Divine Order is the "order of the day." And Divine Order does not follow man's ideas of sequence at all. You have set up certain unspoken, subconscious rules to give "sequential order" to your experience. The forces of God do not have to follow sequence to have organization. Therefore, it is important that once the process is initiated to a critical point, then you must trust in its completion of itself without the ego control so familiar to each of you. This is imperative, lest you monkey wrench your own dream.

Our co-operative effort and it is that, must begin, continue and end with focus on a completed goal. It is the composite of dreams of what a Utopian world would be like, one that each would truly like to experience that will bring this to pass. This is the opposite of the resistance that is expected. How much time do each of you spend in this "utopian daydreaming" process? Survival daydreams are more the norm in the group that we are depending upon for this formative process. Granted such a thing as easy earth compatible energy sources are a part of that dream, for luxuries of easy living are not appealing sacrifices for freedom of oppression. This is what is automatically supposed will be the cost of such change. Would a new paradigm of experience be without comforts? Different comforts probably, but I doubt anyone will feel any regrets for having given up the present situation. This again is the "resist or be shoved backwards" thought process that must be abandoned. That you want what will make your experience even better is a given, and it should be assumed. It must also be assumed there may be a short period necessary to endure in order for this change to happen, but it can be shorter than you might imagine. When this pivotal project is accomplished, our help is not only allowed, it is mandated. It is the beginning "think tank" discussions that will bring about the beginning of the change of expectation to an ever-expanding group. Think of a stone tossed into a pond. The ripples reach out to a effect a greater and greater area. We call it a critical point, you refer to it as the "100th monkey theory". Think of the counter thought group as having to send the ripples in from the outside to the middle. Remember they are creating what is not in accordance with the laws of God. Their concentration is toward containment while your focus is toward rippling outward. Now, which one do you think works better? When these ripples meet what happens? If you are using the same pond water, which one is likely to overwhelm the other, especially if the stone that is dropped is becoming larger and larger in what might be interpreted to be slow motion?

Remember there are vibrational effects that are and will be brought into being that cannot be observed by you. Each time the thought pattern is focused toward the goal, it becomes further intensified. As it intensifies, it becomes more magnetic and attraction begins to build. You are not likely to surprise any of the contacts. What you are most likely to hear is that it has been in their thoughts already, but they just hadn't made the effort to follow through with its implications. The process will become appealing and challenging when you begin to dream of ways to use the mechanisms put in place for the use of those of opposite intentions. Doesn't that sound intriguing? Rather than destroy and resist, it might be possible to use some of what they have in place for your own intentions. You have focusing powers that are capable of many things when there is group participation and a few innovations of your own can be added. Remember the pipe that sends vibrations to the crops in the fields? Ever wonder what else it is capable of doing? You might be surprised. Even the sound embedded in Dan Carlson's music tapes for the growth of plants might be interesting in the presence of their focused vibrations. Just a thought or two about what you already have available.

No. 6

The light begins to change its focus as the window changes in what might be considered depth, as layers of intentional activity will be added. The focus becomes more intense in the area on which it is aimed. Now this can be an advantage as it can bring the focus to a greater clarity. That the cloak of darkness appears to you to be getting more intense can have its positive aspects. The closing of the noose is not as unobserved by the masses as you might think. Intuitive feelings are becoming aroused. The critical mass of awareness is being aroused and the other side is well aware of this. Remember there is a weak link within their plan. They are going to demand that their army of militia turn on their own people, indeed their own friends and family. That is a key point on which there will be reactions that they cannot predict. This allows openings in their plan. They seem minor to you in your consideration, but these can be used to great advantage for sometimes a moment is all the focus of Light may need.

Ours will not be a plan of resistance. It will be the lifting up of a vision into manifestation through the minds of many. When the picture of what has been carefully planned for them is repulsive enough to their imaginations, don't you think that they will turn with enthusiasm to a vision that thrills them? Remember there will be those who will choose otherwise. There will be a division. There will be enough that have been either won over or will be lost in the desire of continuing to experience the menu which has been fed to them in the media barrage directed at them. This will be a point you will have to deal with, as will all that join in this plan for transcending the decayed into the new birthing opportunity. All will not choose to join, and here you must recognize the free choice of experience given to each. It is not so much hardening your heart toward them as an attitude of allowance. Remember there is no death. Only the end of an experience and eternity is incomprehensible. It is not for any of you to judge what the experiences of each individual means to the completion within each Soul. The Soul draws to itself a composite and makes of these experiences patterns that dazzle the imagination. The dance of duality, darkness and Light as you will, are part of the play.

You must not become disheartened at any time, for there will be those who will surprise you. It is for you to keep your eye on the vision and to watch it unfold into creation from your limited perspective. That too will be fascinating. How will you know? It will be difficult in the birthing phase, for in the beginning the process of a babe hardly looks like anything but a maze of dividing cells, with no apparent organization. At the critical point, all that miraculously changes into a form. Then the challenge of preventing an abortion will become a dual focus. However, that too shall be handled. Remember this: as you begin to help yourselves, more and more co-operation from various forms of manifested Light can assist in ways you, and even I, cannot imagine and may never be privy to know about. It is the focus on the vision that shall attract this assistance toward success.

We can continue to present this information to you, but there can also be discussion. Questions can be asked as long as they are pertinent to the process at this point. No divining allowed. Just focus on one stage at a time. What your continuing roles shall be as the plan unfolds will be revealed as each day arrives. There is no already existing vision except in a dim outline that is set up by the influence of the Universal Laws. At the time of filling in these outlines, those will be made known to the founding parents in very simplistic terms. KISS will be the "order of the day" for the entire project. How is that going to be possible within the contributions to the vision by many? Trust the process. The planet is experiencing on an entirely different level than it was when the founding fathers of the U.S. followed this same path. Note this time it is "founding parents," and that in itself is a raising of the level of experience. Both energies shall be present and it shall make for a doubled energy focus. Though women knew the last time and supported as allowed, theirs was not a contributory role except as an outside influence. Neither shall dominate, for the vision must move beyond such selfishness and bring about a synergistic wholeness.

At this point, you must not concern yourselves with the manifestation of their plan. You know of it, you are expecting it and so it must be ignored. Your focus must be on the moment and what is to be done. If that which you do now puts you in danger, perhaps you should begin laying plans for doing something different. Not yet in this moment, but soon. Perhaps this surface activity cycle is drawing to a close. It is only a suggestion to be considered, though you already have toyed with it. We leave it to your discretion. Corporate business will be allowed for activities that do not make big waves. Opportunities shall appear for your consideration.

Travel shall be safe for a time yet. If you miss a plane or a flight is canceled take it within your stride. There may be many reasons apparent in retrospect as to why you were not to be on a particular mode of transportation. When travel is no longer safe, you will know. The focus of your intent now is to work within the activities of the parenting process.

No. 7

There is much being done to bring into concrete experience the truth of the statement that the unseen world is more real than the one that is seen by the mass consciousness on the planet now. These concrete demonstrations of the nature of this unseen causal effect are not only stimulating awareness, but bringing forth the opportunity to use this knowledge to encourage the visioning of the process that together we are beginning to bring forth. (How is that for talking all the way around the subject?) It helps to bring it out of the realm of wishing into the realization that there is a way to counter their methods without adopting them. The work to be done is not at this 3rd dimensional level of resistance, but as I have emphasized before, at the causal level of creating what is another focus entirely. The reality of the possibility of this process has already been demonstrated in fields that indicate these processes can be adopted and focused in accordance with what is needed. The already proven success of these "theories" adds the inspiration needed to bring forth the birthing activity. It is recommended that the "messages" be held for those who would be encouraged to join the birthing process in the immediate future. These people will quickly see the correlation, and of course some are already in the awareness of some or all of its contents. A basic awareness of both sides of the forces present is needed and that information is available and it is necessary that it be known to those selected as the parents of this process. It is a human weakness to assume that what is known to one, is also known to all. Details are not necessary, but an overview would be most helpful with an available "catalog" of well documented information for those desiring a more comprehensive understanding in areas not familiar to them.

The processes mentioned in the "message" are of course known to those engaged in this broad research and these strive to be merely known, but not to create a situation that will bring public awareness. At that point their existence is a threat to the powers that assume invincibility. These would then be in a precarious situation as the noose tightens. Their importance cannot be stressed enough. This is the reality check needed to assure the success of the understanding that these higher vibrational realities need to be "pulled" into the experience of this planet. As the "message" reveals, the comfort zone under threat can bring violent reactions, not only in the circles of the opposition, but among the general public. The opposition at its highest levels knows that it is threatened by a possible collapse of its operation from the inside out. The mass consciousness is merely reacting in a "Pavlov's dog" fashion. Possibility thinking is not acceptable.

Herein lies the need for careful movements within the project until the critical mass is reached. This is why the approach to the plan must be by word of mouth to known individuals who then take the responsibility of approaching those who they know have the proper sympathetic awareness and desire to see the situation change. The ability to identify with the change to be made at levels behind the "5 senses" experience must be paramount in the beginning parenting process. It isn't the number of people involved at this stage, but the quality of the awareness that is important. The ability to possibility think, the openness to expansion of awareness and the ability to assimilate and postulate into new synthesis, the known and unknown, is of critical importance. In other words, choose carefully. With that step clearly in mind, the proliferation will take care of itself. The clarity of the first combinations will set the stage for the entire process.

No. 8

It is interesting that the power of thought has brought us to a meeting point of consciousness. This is a process of intent focused toward a mutual purpose. It is this bringing together of purposeful intent that is the magic of shared manifestation. It is evident in the perceived world that surrounds you in both its positive and negative forms. Now the plan is to raise that process to a higher level, to engage known processes to further your exploration of the process of manifestation. It is a matter of intention that brings forth the knowledge to be able to do this from a vantage point of awareness of the essential elements to ensure completion. This need not be done through blind faith in an unknown process. This would encourage an attrition rate that would ensure failure. It is a matter of making the data available to the conscious awareness and then allowing it to percolate. The inspiration for application will come forth into understanding. Manifestation is not a haphazard, lucky combination of synchronistic meetings. There are specific already existing procedures in place available to be used. It is a matter of bringing these purposefully into the awareness and then the creative imaginations will trigger the appropriate applications. "The luck of the draw" is simply too risky to be relied on in this project.

Here again the stress remains on the careful choices for the parenting operation. It is not desired to belabor this point, but it is awesomely important.

Ours is a most important combination of massaging your consciousness (plural) and stimulating your concerns without bringing forth panic. We are finding this to be a skill that is most rewarding. It is indeed bringing about the desired results. You are not the only ones to which this process is being applied. Just know that all that can be done from this level is being done. It is in the actual movement from the point of inertia that will allow this behind the scene help to aid in bringing forth the manifestation of the plan. Remember the birthing process begins with the dance of desires and culminates in an apparent miracle through processes that go on for the most part beneath the level of conscious awareness. These processes are not haphazard, but proceed within exacting synthesis of multiple complicated interactions. If there was an original plan for this commonplace happening, then don't you think that a plan for one as important as this one is also in place? If you do not need to be aware of the functions relating to the birth process of a child to complete itself, then do you need to know of all the processes that will happen in this project? The human birthing process would not happen if certain physical actions did not take place to initiate its beginning.

What is being emphasized here is that you understand you will not shepherd the whole process to its conclusion. Neither do we want you to think you will be left out of the project once it is initiated. Indeed, you will be included in ways that are not in the most freewheeling of your imagination at this moment. In this case, we encourage you to trust the process and continue to be available, for you are all needed. You did not sign on for a short-term assignment.

Let us continue now by moving on to other subjects that are of course related. It is important to keep a balance in this stretch of your understanding of this commitment to the transcendence of the planet and its inhabitants. Know that this is hardly a single handed commitment, but the agreed upon commitment of countless numbers of beings who are not strangers to the process. In this case, the energy of this particular planet has reached a level of heaviness that is challenging to say the least. But after all, you must know that all of you thrive on challenge and this is no exception. However, this time it is not a game, for failure would have serious implications beyond the mere suffering of incarnated beings. This of course is known to you at your deepest levels, so it is not meant as a threat. In this case, we are allowed greater discretion to assist and we are stretching it to the utmost in order to initiate the beginning of this project. Much planning has gone into the methodology with contingencies covered for the art of improvisation is not limited to 3rd dimensional experience.

It is known that a certain lack of sincerity exists within the realms of those who present themselves as leading the resistance to the planned changes. In this case, either these will find themselves involved in other activities or you will have a distinct knowingness regarding the appropriateness of their inclusion. The identity of some of these might come as a surprise, but again you are connected to a point now that you will know in the moment when it is necessary to be cautious. Most of what is included today in this contact is known to you, it is as yet not possible to reveal detail for two reasons. The proper sequences are not yet in place and this line of communication is not yet at a level for these to come through. All possible is being done to prepare this last phase so that there will be a coordination of these elements. Again, we ask your patience and that you trust the process, redundant as it may seem at times. As you say, just hang in there.

No. 9

The situation is this. Time is the primary element used to recognize placement within the 3rd dimension. However, the veil between dimensions is thinning. As the awareness grows of the availability of 4th and even 5th dimensional processes for usage in this 3rd dimensional realm, this veil will begin to thin even more. The new focus must include elements of the higher dimensions. How to do this! Thought moves between dimensions as long as the thought is within those dimensional parameters. 3rd dimensional parameters allow for interfering with the development of others. It allows for the forcing of one will upon another. Above that dimension, all are allowed freedom to develop without this interference. Personal responsibility is the keynote of existence. Contrary to the mass consciousness appearance of the lack of development of this level, it is there, simply smothered by the barrage of mind control techniques. However, those techniques are not as successful as it might appear. If these were, then the massive physical control that is being put in place would not be necessary. If these were, then there would be no problem of what to do about what they see as overpopulation. There would be masses of people following like lemmings into the sea. What is becoming a rising tide, is the ground swell of feeling of people longing for this personal freedom.

Through the moving of jobs from your country, people have found that they can create for themselves new opportunities, however nebulous they may be within the "communications" dream of non-production. This success within planned failure has tweaked the creative urge within many thus the proliferation of home based businesses. It is this glimmering of personal success that has sparked a surge within even the most oppressed of the beings in your country, meaning the welfare recipients. This information has not stayed within the boundary of this country. It has always been alive in countries of great poverty. If it were not, more would have starved long ago.

This longing for freedom will be fanned into a blaze by the dream and its simplicity. It will be this new conception that will lift the spirits of those who will hear, and the lift will be literal. The inner prayer of the longing hearts shall be answered and their reaction to it will not be stopped. It can't be reached by third dimensional methods, for those who try to apply them will simply be left as helpless as was the dark plan for the people. Once the critical point of awareness is reached, support of the new paradigm will take the planet forward as a whole. The "ascension" of the new age dreamers is one of individual flights into the clouds, but this shall be a planetary change. Your bible mentions two standing in a field and only one is taken. The person who wholeheartedly believes in the dream shall accompany the dream.

The parents of this dream must have the understanding, that 3rd dimensional parameters must be transcended and thought must be focused into the higher expectations of a new dimension. Trust in the personal responsibility of its citizens will be the key to the foundations of that new perception. It is the password, so to speak, for entry into this experience. Honesty and forthrightness are practiced without question. Your 23rd psalm translation misrepresented this by the word "righteousness" which was given the meaning of judgmental attitude, in particular, the actions of others. Instead, it was meant that each was to be responsible to live rightly within the *personal* focus of their life attitudes and actions. This would result in finding that games of inappropriate action will not work if no one else will play by those rules. There can be no victims and no martyrs if no one will play that game. This may sound naive considering the chaos around you, but that is the difference. That is the leap that must be made, through the assumption that humanity has a critical mass that is ready to assume this shift in perception. The profit motive at the expense of all others has not lead to Utopia. Man in true prospective is a radiant being, meaning created to give outward the expression of the Creator's Love, not to live as a usurper with only the intent of drawing all toward himself as depicted by the material experience. The experiment of this has left him hollow and unfulfilled. This shall be the opportunity to experience what will satisfy and fill his heart cup to running over.

How can you paint this vision with the color of emotion that shall magnetize all that hear it and catch them up into movement toward it? Intent shall be the alchemical ingredient, and the Creator's Love of his children shall spread butter upon the path, to convert an old adage to a different focus. It can be done, it shall be done, on that you can place your life's focus and trust. The etheric winds of change are in motion and the momentum is building. Do you think there is anything that can stand against the Creator of the game in the first place? It cannot be so. Welcome to the winning side! Now isn't that a wonderful greeting?

This seems like a logical place on which to end this exchange of thought. Open your hearts and feel the love that is given to you for your trust and acceptance of our combined path in this marvelous adventure of adventures. How will we top this one? It is not for us to know, yet.

No. 10

The movie, "The Siege", contained heavy subliminal messaging. Just one point, remember that it used the constitution to resolve the difficulty. However, their intention is to use executive orders so that there is no constitution for where will there be a judge with authority to stand against the dark organization. The realization of that will quickly demoralize the people. That was another sleeping pill of greater magnitude than you realize. Asking for shielding and for discernment was quite effective and it will be most helpful to use it as the situation progresses. It is something that will need to be done by each and not something that can be done for a group by one person. Again we go back to the law of individual responsibility.

It will be interesting for you to know that the planetary consciousness is changing. Let us compare this to a breathing pattern. It is as though the planet is changing its steady intervals of inhale and exhale to an irregular pattern of a deeper inhale as compared to the exhale as a gathering of internal energies. That is an area of our discussions that has not been covered. The planet too shall participate in the plan to change the situation. Remember that all manifestation at all levels is the result of the projection of thought into the malleable ethers (your name for creative potential), and that thought is interactive within itself in the ability to maintain balance.

You can perceive that you are beginning to experience a focus of change in a cooperative energy vibration. This has the potential to synchronize the inhabitant consciousness to blend with that of the planet as a whole. Perhaps this will allow you to begin to understand why we belabor the point of the importance of the parenting cells being of the consciousness that will produce this blending vibratory ratio. There shall be a quickening of the latent emotional connections to the planetary consciousness, not to the suffering on her part because of mankind's infliction of selfishness and greed, but to the area of conscious desire for change to a new and different experience. Remember this is not the first civilization to experience here and you do not know the history of these previous scenarios. Just as you experience and learn, so also is this repeated in the evolution of the planet as a whole. Here you begin to see the damming up of energy that is occurring now. When a hole in this dam is released in a direction that the whole of this energy can blend into cohesively, then there can be a release that will flush away the infection and bring about a healing of marvelous proportion. Just as a journey begins with the first step, so also this begins with the tiny hole in the dam by the formation of the first cells of the birthing process.

It is not yet clear exactly what the planetary involvement will be as it depends upon the blend of energy that parents the part of the process that is contributed by humanity. It is the key that unlocks the whole of the project. We, of course, have observed various scenarios of possible energy combinations similar to your computer projections and find that each brings forth a vastly different combination of possible reactions. Each leads to a similar end conclusion, not only in different combinations of similar elements, actions and reactions, but in different elements, actions and reactions entirely. Therefore definite conclusions cannot be made even from this perspective. Isn't that interesting? We think so. Thus, once the selections are made and the first cells begin to act in the creation of the possible "dream" scenarios it still will not be possible to project much of clarity until it, the dream scenario, becomes clear in the minds of these groups as a whole.

Can we guide this process based on our test projections? We wish we could, but that would be unacceptable interference. In this case, the guidance will have to come from a higher Source than we are. There is little doubt that the Highest of High is most interested in what is happening here and that Source will be available for exactly the help needed. These miniature planetary think tanks will be allowed to play with possibilities, but the request for High Source help will no doubt have much powerful input into the completion of the process. I can assure you that this level knows mankind to its very core and will guide the process, but there must first be the movement beyond desire into active thought projection for the purpose of manifesting this new experience. After the creative dreaming of possibilities, then follows the purposeful focus process to place the skeletal outline in place. The great reward will be the painting in of the details with the experience of that which you will have created. The joy of this part of the process shall be wonderful indeed.

No. 11

The mantra of this project must be "In God We Trust!" You cannot trust manifested mass conscious beliefs. The seeds of death for your fellow human beings are beyond the planted seed stage and into sprouting and rapid growth. There is but one "salvation" from this trap. It is in the service to and total trust in the way <u>through</u> this situation. There is not a way out; there is only the way through. The subtle difference is not apparent, but is indeed of great importance. Out implies resistance, through implies movement through toward a greater goal lying beyond. Just as one does not get out of a mountain pass, but must move through it, so must you identify with the subtly different application. Mankind falls into the dream of a great leader being raised up in consciousness to "lead" it out of this or any other dilemma. It cannot be. It must be by the inspiration of visualizing a way of Life that fills the empty void of their consciousness that the political, scientific and religious dogma of the past and present has brought to each. The realization that only their own desire to participate, following a personal conscious decision, will lead them through this experience to what awaits beyond.

Man is an adventurous being, loving challenge. This desire for personal adventure has been diverted into the false desire for safety, the assurance of limited risk (insurance). Remember the navy posters that appealed to the young men by offering the adventure of sailing to unknown ports, only to end up with wooden guns guarding a metal fenced enclosure such as did Bill Cosby? Military combat is represented as an "adventurous" activity, but it is not on a personal responsibility level. Each activity is planned out not by the individual, but by the layers of officers. Yet military heroes are those that in the moment of need act on their own to accomplish a deed at great risk to themselves. For the public at large risk is left to such things as the risk of death on snowboards, skiing on possible avalanche areas, swimming in possible rip tide areas, climbing steep mountains, etc. These too shall soon be cut off, to further stifle the soul into greater limitation. The pent up feelings are then channeled into destructive outlets of wars, gangs, rape, pillage and other activities contrary to the purposes of manifested Life. This leads mankind from its original purpose of finding the connection and the path of return to the Creator.

You already know this, so of what point is this discussion? This is so that you might recognize the feelings that are prevalent, especially among the young people. What change is experienced when you remember that there is a plan to lead the human experience in the opposite direction, into the Promised Land of true personal adventure in dealing within the realms of personal self. This is what is being experienced in the greater manifested reality. It is but an enlarged mirror image of what is taking place within.

The identified 300 are but 300 focused tricks of these distorted egos given free rein through the manipulation of their minds. All effort has been made to assist individuals on the personal level to realize this. Now, the manifestation of the "evil" (misunderstanding and misuse) must be dealt with by the extreme method of bringing forth a movement to halt this process on the same level as has been achieved by the misused egos of the dark ones. This has occurred by the process of the ego empowering itself into areas contrary to its purpose. This process has reached proportions of imbalance, which endanger the integrity of the Galaxy/Universe. Extreme measures have been sanctioned by the Creator to bring this back into balance.

Because of the Love of the Creator for his fragments, all possible means to return these into equilibrium are being used. Some shall indeed be denied manifested Life experience for what you would term long periods of time, as many opportunities to turn from their focus of separation have been given them. Others shall continue their lessons in other situations for they are but innocently duped during the experience they chose by incarnating here.

Those who have true intent and purpose shall move through the experience by their choices of participation within bringing forth this manifestation of the new creation scenario. This group-focused demonstration will carry a power of transformation that shall be thrilling indeed. It is a gift of the Creator. This shall be a blessing and a gift of Grace through a profound Love focus beyond all previous experience. Through this shall the raising of this planet occur, its transcendence shall ripple outward through all of creation allowing new levels of experience. The transcending participants will enjoy the rewards of participating within this completion. The mercy and grace available within the Loving focus of the Creator is included within the infinity of "His" Love. The finite mind is unable to fathom this, but there shall be an expansion of the ability to encompass this to a greater degree within this focus of human experience and expression within the changing of the dimensions. But even the dimensions shall change through this scenario so that all consciousness shall be thrilled by new experience and be further awakened.

Now, does the greeting "Welcome to the winning side" carry new meaning? Indeed! The intent of these messages is to deepen the resolve and to give all possible support to the tasks upon your plates. May your hearts be inspired to continue your devoted participation with the blessings of all beings of Light involved in this project. Your bible has a saying, "and she pondered this in her heart." An apt way of putting it. May you open your consciousness to experience the Love that surrounds, inspires and protects you on this day! Indeed!

No. 12

We find it interesting that the forces of evil are putting forth a dual effort. The ethnic and racial differences between individuals and groups are being stressed and agitated while at the same time you are being forced into a "one world government". This, of course, is not without planning. It is for the purpose of creating chaos and confusion within the psyche. In actuality, this serves our purposes also. It is a great deal easier to create change from chaos than it is to bring it about within a stable, static environment. There are a great many planets that are highly developed within the adaptation and adoption of the Universal Laws. If this is such a wonderful state, then the question is why focus the opportunity of transcendence of such magnitude as is being hinged upon this process through a planet that is in the gross experience of this one. The answer is that it is the chaotic energy that offers the greatest potential for this particular process. That which you call God has not "created" your dilemma, but it is His Creation and certainly he can participate in the potential that it offers, much to your benefit we might add.

We are offering as many perspectives to this situation as possible, so that you might have as much understanding as possible. It is necessary that you rise above the stressful awareness that much suffering is being experienced by many of your fellow human beings that have incarnated upon this planet now. This is so that you can perceive from a level of perception that will allow you to have a "God's eye" view from which to conceive your plans. The conception of the "one world government" by the opposition also serves a purpose. Many of the incarnated beings have indeed put aside the nationalistic views they once had and are thinking in terms of global inclusiveness. The project plan will be one that will appeal to more than those of the USA. Of necessity it must be a plan of planetary scope. Necessarily, its beginning is focused here in the U.S.A., but the total picture must be of global intent.

There will be a particular intensity of chaos that will be the pivotal time for change, either for them or for us. Thus the timing for the creation and birthing into the awareness of this plan or dream as we have previously called it is critical. In the nebulous unformed stage of the process, the word dream seems more appropriate in that a plan indicates something already in thought form. This is not yet the case and also keeps it in the mindset of a more playful and creative format. It does not carry the heavy responsibility emphasis for the participating groups. It is intended to promote a maximum of possibility thinking in the broadest possible ways. In the beginning phases, there must be no thoughts of boundaries. Remember that we are not to consider the actions or the reactions of the other side. We are going to be dreaming within little known possibilities; therefore all things are possible. The contingent plans of the other side can only work in their known reality. You are going to be setting up a reality that is far outside anything that they have even considered. It is this level of creativity that we are striving to encourage you to reach. This is creativity that will supersede and stretch beyond the current reality. Can you do this? Of course! Why do you think we tried out possible contingency plans? These are available for you in the etheric fields, not for the intention of you to choose one of them, but merely as beginning points for you to exercise your imaginations. Remember your imagination is the entry point to the "mind of God" which is infinite potentiality. The invocation of His Presence when "two or more are present," is true to a degree you limited ones have not yet perceived.

Any preconceived ideas individual members of these groups may have considered are to be used only as beginning points. No applicable possibility has as yet been conceived. This may challenge some egos in the early stages of participation, but this is a critical time in the education of egos. These observer parts of 3rd dimensional existence must be encouraged to enter into the imaging process and through this they will experience their true purpose. Even the ego will find joy within this process for in experiencing its true role it shall desire to experience more of this joy. Indeed, it is not an entity of separate identity, but is a very active aspect of the human experience that has received far too much emphasis within the complex union of Soul extension energies. Yet we must credit this distortion with the creation of this planetary opportunity, so from that perspective, this activity has contributed in its own unique way. God can turn anything into a purposeful synergy to benefit the whole. More faith on the part of mankind to the reality of this Truth would be of great assistance to them in this project.

The understanding of how individuals experiencing this incarnation fit into the cosmic scheme of things is a little like reading a corporate organization chart. However, this one would be amazingly complex for you to understand in totality for it does not follow the logical responsibility pattern of heavy at the top. Can you conceive of equality from top to bottom of something that has no top and no bottom? Stretches the logic of it, does it not? Does it make sense? Of course it does when linear sequence is not an essential parameter. How could a group accomplish anything without sequence being necessary? Quite well I assure you. How can things manifest without a beginning or an end? Amazingly, you think that it must begin as it appears in the formation of the baby. What appears to be the process in 3rd dimension begins in the etheric. The unseen part of the process is a complete being and already exists at the moment of conception. From completeness in one dimension, it manifests in your reality. A flower was not brought into manifestation from a plant cell, but was conceived in its wholeness not only in appearance, but also in process.

Will your group be responsible for the conception of the process of what needs to be accomplished to change this earthly dilemma? Why do you think so many "etheric" beings are present? We are here to help you with the unseen processes needed. Once the skeletal outline is in place, in a form that will bring the desired results, then you will not be able to imagine the activity that will take place, all focused toward a "splendid moment of creation." Are you being supported through this process? You had better believe it. But—it all hangs on the initiation by humanity of actively creating its own destiny through changing its perception of the ideal, in fact because of the chaos and confusion, in the creation of <u>an ideal.</u>

May the energy that awaits the initiation of the process in small part fill your experience. You are much appreciated and all possible support encompasses you this day. Be of good cheer as you go about your seemingly mundane tasks. Nothing in the lives of humans shall remain mundane for long.

No. 13

The energies as projected by those that would insnare the inhabitants of Earth in their plans to change the destiny of this planet moves in ever tightening circles as they attempt to incorporate the wheels within wheels that constitute a partial understanding of the cycles of creation. They are, oh so, careful to check each cog so that none are out of sequence. Linear thought is still the basis of their game for there is no spiraling toward evolutionary change. Evolution is the term given to change in your language. There is a lack of understanding what the process is. What are they evolving toward? The enslavement of the remaining population is the goal, but for what purpose? A stagnant Utopia? What makes them think that the Universe could or would support them in that process? To rebel against the process of creation is one possibility, but to maintain themselves outside of the focus of Creation would incorporate an ever-escalating process within its totality, and it is doomed to failure. To hijack a planet is one thing; to create an anti-universe is indeed grandiose, for there would be no other way. From where would that kind of energy come? Do they plan to hijack an entire universe? I doubt that which you call God is so impotent as to allow that.

Again I say "welcome to the winning side!" This may seem impossible to believe in view of the above comments. From one perspective that kind of arrogance is humorous. Of course it is not for those experiencing the day to day flexing of the muscles of their power and viewing it from the basis of 3rd dimensional experience. To bring a transition in the human consciousness, the largest view possible is necessary for those who would envision this change. Perhaps change is not the best term, for it implies merely readjusting that which already exists. This has been tried before in other opportunities to outwit the adversary. Obviously it didn't work or you would not be facing this situation. This time you must go a step farther in your refusal to play the game according to their rules. You must change your tactics completely so as to cause their plans to be as impotent as they have schemed to make you. You must transcend those plans. Much ado has been made for "ascending" and for "rapture". Well, this indeed shall be our version of that, except "Jesus" will not do it for you. You must do more than claim to be a "Christian". It will not be necessary to get your hands dirty in the blood of your enemy. Neither shall you be required to turn the other cheek and look away as he does as he wills, for you shall have plans of your own that will employ God's methods that you have until now forgotten. The Armageddon of their vision shall never occur. There shall be an Armageddon, but it shall be played out on a different field and there shall be no conflict as has been envisioned for you.

Your desire for delivery and your will to thwart these puffed up antagonists of Creation shall be guided to fruition along paths of remembering. This shall bring forth the elements of the spiral of evolution that are missing from their carefully laid plans. Fear not, for you have on your side the energies that create solar systems, galaxies, universes and cosmos, indeed All That Is. Could you ask for more support? It is not that it has been lacking during the previous opportunities, but that the cleverness and focus of the antagonists have planned carefully to bring this action to a planned point of implementation at the moment of coinciding cycles. This they believe to be a point of vulnerability. Indeed, however, at those points of cycle endings, the Creator has planned opportunity for His holographic fragments to take advantage of the spiral acceleration that is potentially present. Attention is energetically focused toward that process which allows for those who will to take advantage of the opportunity.

This has been a very simplistic explanation of this unique situation. Indeed history will be written in the annals of this planet. The pot boils, the steam builds and the Universe holds its breath as the moment approaches. Could the process fail? No, but the degree of advantage taken within the opportunity shall affect all within this Universe. Remember that the Creator focus uses all within the flow of ever moving energy in Creation. Chaos is especially pregnant with opportunity for change. It is not to put pressure on you that this knowledge is being shared, but to add to your understanding of the opportunity that is being brought into the situation that appears so hopeless. You must have your eyes open and use your ability to observe and analyze the actions that are taking place about you. The avatars of the past have planted the seeds of understanding that lie dormant within human awareness. It is time to stimulate these seeds into sprouting and growth toward a maturation of 3rd dimensional experience. Those that can accept this stimulation will and those who cannot shall be given other opportunities. Shall any fragments be destroyed? All fragments of the Creator's awareness must be accounted for. Those aspects that have chosen to experience extreme imbalance are put into a space that is something like exile. It is not a burning hell as used to frighten you into submission, but a space of separation to consider and to contemplate. Beyond knowing that this experience exists, it is unnecessary to know more for it is between those and their own inner Spirit.

Will those that brought this to bear and those that choose not to share the opportunity be judged? Judgement has been a word used to conjure up failure and guilt. Release that concept. It is another of the tools used to control you, for instead at the closure of this experience there is a releasing process. A review and a time for the Soul (source of each human focused into experience) to assimilate these experiences into the matrix of its totality. The experiencing focus cannot measure the impact of its life experience upon the matrix of the totality of that which focused it. It is that which focuses contemplating itself. It would be self-condemnation for judgment to take place. Self-condemnation does not exist in higher dimensions. There is a world of difference between self-condemnation and Self-contemplation. Condemnation and judgement are synonyms.

This message is given in Love. It is for enlightenment within the experience of communion with the flow of Creation. It is intended to bring you to the awareness of being within its flow. That is exactly where you are.

No. 14

A new day begins in the lives of those residing upon this planet! Does this sound beyond imagination? No indeed! The desire for what is entirely different creates a new vibratory opening. This indicates there have been others who have contemplated this possibility. The pieces of the puzzle have not been in their proper places before. In order for the chances of success to be at their greatest potential, certain sequential events and circumstances must be in pivotal positions. The mass consciousness of the planet has to reach both a particular level of the knowledge of the truth and a level of frustration within the feelings of resistance to recognizing the changes coming upon them. There is present within those with the advantage of media communication the awareness of the repressive process, but as yet they are in the denial stage. Even that is giving way to the suffocating feeling of the Inner Presence that is being psychically repressed.

You think of this as being a mind control game they are playing, but I tell you it is deeper than that. It is designed to imprison the Inner-Self, which then causes the brain to slow, and the mental sleep process appears as a symptom. If it were only a process of stupor at the mind level, then you could have all been drugged into sleep long ago. That is not the object of the process. What would that prove to the Creator? What is at stake is the proof of superiority through the capture and diversion of the Soul energy and the enslavement of those of particular energy matrix. At a certain point of the negative plan, those who have served them so faithfully will be among the first to be abandoned for they have already proved their corruptibility. Their ideal slave has a different matrix entirely.

If the plan is to continue the game into larger foci of power, then of what use are sleeping slaves? How then do the planners of this escapade locate the ones of value to them? Would it be the ones that do not fall under the spell of their concerted efforts? Just whom do you think that identifies? Indeed, the stakes are high for each of you personally. Does this description fit? Why else have you been allowed to continue in the business of pointing fingers at who they are and what they are doing? These comments are not to instill fear into you, but to give you the greatest possible understanding of the situation that is now in front of you, indeed upon your plates. You have no place to go except through this experience.

This is a short message, but it is one to be added to the previous knowledge. Let us consider it the leavening of the bread to lift your intent to an even greater focus. Know that all this is given with the greatest of Love, for you are more valuable to the Light than to them. You are our key to the lock that now holds the totality of this planet in prison.

No. 15

There is within the organization of those with negative intentions for this planet and their contacts with the extra-terrestrials masterminding the entirety of this planned raping of Earth, a good deal of miscommunication. Each has their separate agenda. Each has plans of reaching their clandestine goals at the expense of the other. Herein lies a vulnerable point in their coordinated effort. It is like two pieces in a puzzle that almost, but not quite fit together. Inasmuch as we look at situations in terms of holographic energy composites or matrix pictures, we are able to determine points of vulnerability. So, the point of this is that there is not a united effort within their reality of experience.

The second weakness in their methodology is that of feeding upon the negative energy that is created by the competition that is encouraged within their organization. When a weak link or defection is found or manufactured within the members of their groups, there is almost a feeding frenzy upon that departing energy. It is far more satisfying to them than the same event happening to one of the uninvolved human beings. There is more of their own energy to feed the void of separation that must be maintained in order to continue on their path. They do "eat up" the competition of sporting events. It is this point of clandestine divergence of purpose that is the major object of our attention. This opportunity is just that, our opportunity. Many scenarios to use this to our advantage have been considered. As yet no exact technique has been established, but several possibilities would accomplish the exact effect necessary. What we are saying here is that though your spearheading action is the key in the lock, there are forces at play here that are stacked up behind a dam that holds back energies that dwarf your ability to imagine them. Do not underestimate the importance of your role however, for it is the trigger that releases this energy build up. The forces of Creation are hardly impotent, however they must work within the Laws that create and maintain all of Creation, the magnitude of which only the Energies that allow the potential for creation can encompass. It is as if there is a holding of the breath until your freewill participation begins the shift in the flow of energies.

We on the one hand must encourage and guide you in your desire to fulfill your purpose and assist you to be ready to act so that you can participate in the flow of events that will manifest as this flood of energies is released into movement. Thus we are something like your sports coach, always with our game plan, but having to adjust and figure ways of compensating for the fluctuations in your synchronistic interactions, the movements and intentions of the adversary forces and the freewill aspects of manifested experience. Unfortunately we don't have any recognition for sainted patience in this level of experience. Neither do we have hair to pull out when you surprise us with your personal decisions. The degree of commitment to the changing of the destiny of the planet from how it is now moving, is our only organizational drawing power. The personal motive of the participating individuals is the primary element for inclusion in the beginning consideration of choice of contact. Then other elements of character must be considered. "Blabber mouths" must of course be excluded, but they are not likely to be "available". The last statement may seem a bit crude coming from our dimension of allowance, however it is necessary to make that point clear.

There are many levels of information yet to be considered. Until the primary contacts and discussions are begun, it would be impossible to go further with a cohesive formation of directions for you. There are no planned shots in the dark so to speak. Even your contributions to the totality of this change in your reality must fit within the framework of the Laws of this Universe and of Creation. The Law of Attraction is at the foundation of all other Laws. You shall see this in the coming together of the essential beginning groups and in the final assembly that shall be the cornerstone of this new evolution of experience. Within this pregnant combination of consciousness shall this conception and movement into the birthing process be possible. It is often quoted that there are no accidents, however the freewill ingredient within the evolutionary process certainly contains the seeds of both endless diversity and the leavening of the mix.

We come to the end of this portion of our continuing dialog as this process proceeds in an accelerating mode. Your days are blessed with synchronicity and healing. Love and Light are showered upon you in great amounts in appreciation of your commitment.

No. 16

The time, in your way of reckoning, is coming into a critical numbers of days. We prefer to see it as sequential events. But, since the knowledge of what these events might be is not available to you, time will have to be your way of being aware. We shall try to coordinate time/event correlation with regard to those events that are important for you to be aware of. At the moment, the contact between the parenting groups is the main focus. As things progress, we shall give you such information as is appropriate. The methods of contact between the members must be such that no clear pattern is apparent and the language used must be very vague. As we have mentioned before, certain words must not be used and certainly none consistently. Many of these people have their own pet names for those we often discuss. It would be well to avoid using these, but merely to allude to them or better yet not refer to them at all. This will help to prevent triggering the watch dog systems that monitor you on a regular basis. All systems of contact are monitored. You would do well to get accustomed to that understanding. The more recently a method has come into use, the more easily it is monitored. Unfortunately wire and tomato soup cans just can't fill the bill, so it is with thought and caution that you must use your communication devices. The dilemma of face to face meetings is that if you meet in a public place you will be noticed and if you begin to meet in a clandestine way, you will be noticed. This begins to sound like one of your spy movies, but things are as they are. At this point of course, there is no problem, but as there begin to be meetings among those of you who are apt members of this project, two and two will begin to make sense to them. The "ball" must be passed onward and outward with little return contact regarding the project in a repetitious fashion. No one person or group of persons is to shepherd the project.

All future meetings for business or personal reasons must purposefully exclude any reference whatever to this project. Phone calls, etc. must not be for the purpose of comparing notes. At a certain time the appropriate group shall come together for one meeting in which the ideas for this future experience of mankind shall be blended together. A simple statement of purpose will arrive at identifying the new genre of experience as the focus of this project. This is the time that the choices of to whom the baton is passed must be carefully contemplated by each person and small group. Then each is to make their contact and the purpose explained in a face to face situation where it will be most difficult to be intercepted. Choosing through spur of the moment decisions of appropriate places is best. Your private offices are probably the worst. As I have pointed out before, you are considered entities with special talents and so are of special interest to them. Do not underestimate your stature in their eyes. We know of no other way to remind you of these parameters without setting the stage like a cloak and dagger movie, yet as this is but indeed as a play upon one small stage of Creation, perhaps that is not at all inappropriate. So—play your parts well. Just remember that your timing might not be as perfect as is Bruce Willis' in the movies.

This will come as perhaps a little late since the first of the meetings will have already happened, but that which is focused into this message has already been made known to each of the contacts through other levels of knowing within unconscious awareness. It shall be known to set this parameter. Other levels of your awareness are being instructed in this process in other ways than this.

We are pushing you, but once the process has begun, it shall move more quickly than you imagine for the pressure builds. The understanding of the hell that is planned for each and every human spirit shall cause the focus of a new paradigm to appeal to each contact at a spiritual level to a profound degree. A desire to participate and to help with the solution to the planetary dilemma will be like letting go of a long held breath within the spirit of each. An overwhelming gratefulness shall bring forth the action necessary, for it is said, "God loves a grateful heart". This is true and much can be accomplished through this emotion. It causes an uplifting of the spirit. Certainly those of you who have been in service through the spreading of the Truth to your fellow human beings can use an uplifting. As the acceptance of the future planned for this planet has come into your understanding, the failure of the people to grasp this and their refusal to believe its existence, has caused you to face many a discouraging hour. But, you have each continued on with your spreading of the Truth.

Isn't this a glorious change of focus; the understanding that at long last there is a way, a plan to take shape and the forces of Creation are indeed here to give help? This shall be a pivotal point within each consciousness that will bring a change of attitude and will begin to draw in multitudes of awakening people. It is not that the message of the Truth of what is present and surrounding them will be different at this stage, but there will be a certain underlying attitude that will be the first trip of a trigger to each listening awareness. It will begin to be discussed and the message will pass from one to another in a gathering momentum. No longer will it be limited to only those who listen to the talk shows and lectures. Those who have read and informed themselves shall be asked to inform and explain. Faithful tellers of the awful tale, you are the avatars of this time! But in the new paradigm victim/martyrdom has no place. It is not in the plan to allow that pattern to continue.

This information is for your consideration. May your experience be filled with synchronicities and loving encounters.

No. 17

When the group consciousness came together to create the earth experience as a flow of Creation, the freewill element within the framework was given particular emphasis with the desire to allow the creative element to be given free rein. The hope was that this special emphasis would allow a blossoming of what you might term a utopian experience within the Universal Laws. It was not contemplated that the opposite would be created within the context of this focus. The joy of abundance was seen as a result of the proper placement of those laws at the center of the experience. Instead, the result was that the abundance of materiality became the focus and the concept of "the end justifies the means" became the framework of the distorted use of the Universal Laws.

If the distorted version of the Laws that indeed govern existence in this Universe of projected Thought is all that is known, then how do you create your way through this experience into a new paradigm which is in harmony with the totality of all that does exist in balance? This is the crux of the dilemma. If the earthly focus were created within a group focus, it would seem that a return to that beginning point would be the point to move toward. Picture as a beginning point, a small group of dots coming together into a single larger dot, then this dot expanding outward into a bubble with a focus point in the middle. All of this is within an expanding movement. Next see that bubble as starting to change shape and become an elongated shape which continues to distort into various configurations until it seems to be coming to a bursting point as more and more pressure is focused toward that point. Now, in your imagination, how would you return that configuration to a perfect circle? Think back to the way the circle was created in the first place and repeat the process. Isn't that what we have been recommending? You need not be all knowing upper dimensional beings to do this, for as you come together with the intention of creating this return to balance, you need but invoke the creative process to receive guidance. Believe us when we say that it is through your *concerted* intention that this distortion will be brought into balance.

It is the mass consciousness that controls the shape of the bubble. It exists within a flowing movement of the thoughts of all. As the negative pressure is purposefully pushing the mass consciousness to conform to its distorted thought forms, which are contrary to what supports the existence of the bubble, the mass consciousness begins to react. Certain available connections to the Source of each individual component of mass consciousness begin to enliven, to resonate as if being irritated by this pressure. The awareness of this reaction is causing more pressure to be applied through the methods that have brought the situation to the place that it is now. Think in terms of the bursting point on the bubble. If this bubble were to react, as would one of your balloons, this point would begin to thin and become more vulnerable. What if instead this point which consists of thought which thinks, would instead thicken and react in ways contrary to the apparent laws of the material world? Remember that thought thinking within itself couldn't accept thought that does not fit within the context of creation. Thought contrary to Creation is directional only by focus in what you might think of as requiring great effort. It cannot be released to complete the creation on its own. Thus this process requires that every contingency must be considered and contained within the plan or added to the plan which would then in turn affect the whole of the plan. Do you think this is possible when compared to the realm of thought that can think within itself and know every contingency in less than the blink of an eye? This all thinking thought has one incredible restriction called the "freewill" of the participants. However, when the freewill of the participants comes into resonance through intent and purpose, then indeed all "Creation" breaks loose, so to speak.

Is it as simple as that? What about all the Laws of Creation that have been broken by all those within the mass consciousness? Isn't each of them required to repent and give up all their erroneous thinking? Come now, isn't that what experiencing is all about? You have forgotten something. Each of you is thought manifested into 3rd dimensional energy! If thought can think within itself, then do you think that it can do that within each individual? It can, but it has the one restriction of "freewill". However, the desire to move through this experience and return this planet as a whole to its rightful place within the Creation is a "freewill" decision. When an internal boiling point is reached within each consciousness by the pressure being applied, don't you think that there shall be a call within each for help from their Creator? There is a point when those who are under the spell of religions that require an intermediary to their God will bypass that belief and undertake a call within themselves that shall awaken the understanding of their true connection. When that reaches a critical level, then that shall join in the new point of focus being formed at the center of the real circle (bubble) of existence which within Creation has always existed. It is a matter of identifying with the real bubble and not the one that is this play on the stage of the mass consciousness.

If that is the case, then why the big deal? Because the play is reality for the mass consciousness and in their freewill it is real and the continued existence of these Soul extensions is in danger of extreme damage with reaction that cannot be explained in 3rd dimensional terms. It is a matter of the realization by enough of these extensions that another reality is within their ability to identify and claim. Perhaps your greeting should be "Welcome to the winning side. Let us identify and claim!"

No. 18

The day begins anew as your planet turns on its axis and mankind sleeps on under the influence of the forces of darkness.

Their plans seem to move in an inexplicable focus of disaster and only the few faithful ones appear to be awake and recording the movement of doom upon this lovely world of green and blue. The magic of the beauty becomes blurred and the very home upon which you depend is shutting down around you and still, if noticed, it is ignored. The final days descend into the abyss while your TV, sports and sleeping potions drug you figuratively and literally.

What now can you few do to stem the tide of blackness as it deepens more and more quickly? Shall we recount again all that you already know and groan and beat upon our breasts, as did the prophets of old and cry out for "God" to save us? Millions are already doing that to a Creator they think ignores their cries to answer their prayers. It is in the perception of victims that desire rescuing that they ask and cannot receive answers to such prayers. Indeed, only those prayers that ask for empowerment within the framework of Creation can be answered. Do you think that the stars stay up in your heavens by casual request of a god being? Indeed not! They are there within the design of balance and mathematical laws that underpin All That Is. Man continues in his mindless begging and blocks the very help he desires by being unwilling to participate except in ways that are contrary to the very Laws that support his unhappy existence. The story of these Laws surrounds them in what remains of nature, but in his misery he blinds himself. The scientific learned ones analyze the components but not the process of Life within the manifested structures of Life that surround them. The mental analysis of the mind deludes him into arrogant belief of his superiority over his surroundings rather than his brotherhood and kinship within it. How can those be helped that are becoming more and more blind to the very process within which they exist?

The victim cannot be rescued, but must pull himself up by his own boot straps and rescue himself by being responsible for his own rescue. Man is made in the essence of his Source. He is a tiny holograph of this Source. A holograph is a tiny fragment of the whole that has the potentiality of projecting the whole from which it came. Though the concept of the holograph has been encompassed in part, it has not been "analyzed" with application to the essence of Life that is within all self-aware beings. It is the refocusing of this fragment toward its source of existence that determines the degree of the totality of the Source that is brought forth into the known reality of each fragment's experience.

If you consider the degree of the focus that has brought forth the planet Earth from the fragment of its Source, you can begin to get the picture. Look at the magnificence of the human body that is the vehicle of your experience here. A vehicle capable of housing a self-awareness that can contemplate its Source if it but will, because that Source contemplates Itself and in so doing fragments Itself so that it can further contemplate Itself through manifestation of experience. Within it is the freewill to do this. Since freewill is the vehicle for this contemplation, then it is manifest within each holographic fragment. This freewill allows for all experience within a further enhancement of this Self-contemplation process. This is the polarity that enables the recognition of that which serves the contemplation process and that which does not, so that the balance of these allows the completion of each exploration into the return of the fragment originally projected to its Source. To follow this process as presented, there is a spiral of understanding as this is contemplated by the mind reading this information. Each fragment returns itself to the Source that projected it. Thus you are led to understand the framework of the process you are within, for each of you is a holographic fragment of the Source of all that is in the process of self-contemplation. Ah, panic, you will become as nothing if you follow the path of the return. Indeed not! With each returning phase toward the Source of your entry into experience, your own self-awareness grows and it becomes greater and greater until you have the absolute potential to be a total equal within the greater Totality of that Source contemplating Itself.

Does that boggle your finite minds? Indeed it should not. It should be the most comforting news that you have ever encountered. Could there ever be a brighter picture of your future ever painted? What possible pleasures could ever compete with a future like that? Let me assure you that there are no fleeting pleasures of the body incarnate that can compare with those that await you as the fragmentary self-awareness begins to ascend the spiral of experience toward the ultimate goal. The problem is bridging the gulf of misunderstanding that has been set as a trap by ones that have become caught up in the distorted misuse of the aspect of freewill. These pitiful ones have become so caught up as to perceive themselves as powerful enough to reach not only total equality with the Totality of the Source of All, but even to can reach a place of Superiority. Even the distorted psychiatric paradigm of your time would consider this insanity if they could but encompass the scheme in its totality.

Within this distorted power grab, it is necessary to have a distorted replica of the process. A counterpart to that which exists. Humanity is but one building block of this, for they cannot create from a negative potentiality. Try as they have, it will not work, so they are left with the process of converting what already exists from what you would term positive into its opposite, a negative counterpart. Now, this is not a recent event in your linear counting process. How much have they accomplished? So as not to overwhelm you completely, let us say that it has reached a critical stage. To allow it to continue would jeopardize more of manifested experience by the Source than is comfortable. Enough to bring a focus of the awareness of this "awesome totality" of Source to bear upon the problem. The potentiality of this Focus for bringing balance back into the totality of the process as explained above is awesome to contemplate, even within the limits of 3rd dimensional perception.

We have attempted to explain before that there is help available, that it is powerful and we have even understated it. However, the key to the release of this awesome force lies within that which has created the situation in the first place. *__FREEWILL!__* If you were not of exceptional value beyond being the vehicle of change, other means of ending this could be employed. The fragment of which each and every individual fragment of that Focus is a portion must be accounted for in order for the balance of all to be maintained. You cannot be simply written off. That would create a flaw that would cause unacceptable repercussions. All fragments must return to the Source from which they were focused (projected) in order for that Source to remain in the balance of wholeness. That is not to say that those that have perpetrated this distorted experience to the extreme will not have some interesting educational experiences, for certainly they shall. Your perception of time does not allow you to contemplate such a process, so do not attempt to do so.

It is important that you gather into your awareness the wholeness of this situation so that you can begin to contemplate the understanding that even those of darkest behavior patterns are valuable to the Source that you call God. They are a part of the totality of all that the word Source implies. Simply telling you that they are a part of "All That Is" has not brought with it comprehension that encompasses the necessary understanding and so another approach to it has been attempted here. A back to basics lesson in your vernacular. Let us hope that this has now been accomplished. If not, perhaps the re-reading of this will bring it about. It is not that we wish a softening of your attitude toward what is being perpetrated which would further their negative cause, but that you understand why simply destroying the whole experiment is not an option, or why just messing up their plans is not enough. The Source, the Big Boss, wants it resolved and who are we to argue? We have this *key issue* to resolve. So, let us get on with it.

No. 19

Around the world there is a greater and greater feeling of unrest. The intuitive aspects of each being begin to awaken for the energy atmosphere of the planet is resonating with the focus of attention placed upon this single planet by the entire galaxy. Your fellow awake and aware co-inhabitants are certainly noticing what is going on here. This is different from the suffocating direct manipulative energies that are being diffused upon your conscious awareness. The galactic attention is coming through energies too subtle to be picked up by mechanistic methods in use by those of focused dark intent. The opposition must attain its ends by employing methods of suppression of the natural expansive movement of thought within manifested form. What is flowing into your mass consciousness from the galaxy that surrounds you is of a natural expansive quality. It is received within the awareness and then follows its expansive nature and arrives exponentially outward into conscious awareness as dreams and sleep patterns that are not restful. The governing factor with regard to the receiving of this galactic message is the degree to which the inner awareness of each individual being has been suppressed. How slow is the vibratory rate of the being? Can it still receive the stimulation of the higher and more rapid vibration of this galactic thought form? This is not a message of condolence that is being sent by sympathetic individuals. That is a trick of the lower dark energies, another of their suppression techniques. Rather, this is a focus of stimulation so that the receptors of Light which hold each in focus may be returned to greater use.

So you begin to see that there are two foci of energy in motion; one of suppression and one of stimulation. We prefer not to use terminology of war here, but it can be noted that the "battle" for this planet is already underway. Not as depicted with carnage everywhere being created by both sides, but in the claiming and the retaining of Soul energies. The one side is planning for many, the other for all. Remember, if one tiny unit of energy is truly destroyed, then the totality of all is lost. The Source of All That Is is expansive in nature. The energy can change form through what appears to be the rise and fall, the birth and death of form, but the energy that is at the very basis of this phenomenon is *always* present.

A polarity always exists within the format of this ever-present energy, however it does not have to be present in the format of what you perceive as evil, dark forces. That opposite polarity is another subject. What you must understand is that what appears to be the opposite polarity in the experience of planet Earth is an aberration, a distorted use of this polarity in energy. It is the exception, not the norm.

The more clearly that you understand what is available to you within the context of this situation, the more easily you will be able to maintain the focus on your purpose within energies that are in motion around and through you. It is easier to succumb to the energies of suppression in some moments of your time than to maintain your focus upon the stimulating energies that are acting within you. The "battle" is not upon the surface of the planet as you have been told, but it is within the individual awareness and it is by definition also within the planetary awareness. It is either understood or misunderstood, that within the planetary awareness, the minds of humanity in combination are the conscious awareness of the planet itself. Therefore the transformation of the planet, earned by her through her repeated motherhood of evolving civilizations, hinges upon the transformation of her current resident civilization. You can begin to understand that the unity of this evolvement process brings forth the potential for misuse. This inner coagulation of energetic purpose is organized for the process of transcendence. The polar opposite conceived one world suppression rather than planetary expansive transformation into higher dimensional (vibratory) experience.

With the presence of so much heavy energy thought exchange between the planetary inhabitants, mind to mind exchange of conceptual understanding has reached very low ebb. This has resulted in a proliferation of mechanized communication, each representing the abilities once in common use by you without a manifested device to make it possible. With the rapid advance of these technologies (devices) through the focus on heavy slow vibratory manifestation, what appears to be marvelous advancement is indeed quite the opposite. It represents a loss of ability to focus the formative, expansive use of the power of thought inherent within all Creation. Sleight of mind is at work again diverting your attention from the potentiality of creating outward from within, through the use of the outer mind activity of analysis and manipulation of your manifested reality. The natural flow would be toward the exploration of the inner awareness and manifesting outward into your realities the greater experiences to be found there. Where do you think the greater people-serving ideas come from? Instead these are being twisted into people-suppressing uses right before your eyes while you fail to observe what is at work. All the while you are watching the show being staged, diverting your attention.

So, now the fun begins in earnest. You are making your final attempts to reach the inner awareness of as many as possible through the last available use of their technologies, but you are also beginning to join forces with the inner energy stimulation. You too are receiving this stimulation. Indeed you are like the repeater stations that your radio stations use. You are serving multiple purposes and you are perfectly aware of doing this within the inner awareness portions of your totality of experience. Trust the process and hold the pole, so to speak. All is far from lost. Welcome to the winning side! Focus and manifest!

No. 20

The glory of your nations fades before your eyes as one by one they are attacked from inside and out. Each is dependent upon the monetary handouts that require handing over mineral rights and other resources as ransom. The money is siphoned off into secret accounts that return to the usurpers as the leaders are deposed or assassinated. The cycles are repeated over and over. The people are abandoned by their governments and so must fend for themselves within situations of less and less available necessities and more and more regulations. Not a pretty picture to behold. So—what now?

Let us again consider possibilities that could bring change to this nightmarish situation. Could it be that the forces behind this situation could be creating causes to culminate this planned suppression of the people of this planet that might involve repercussions that are beyond their ability to control? Could there be small unknown glitches in those plans, which if exploited, could cause outcomes not planned? It is indeed not only possible, but probable. Let us consider Y2K as just one possibility. If indeed all of the technological wonders of the basics of power, water, communications, money, travel, etc. all depend upon computers to operate, then so also must the military and conspiratorial communication systems and other wonderful mechanisms of planned use. All of these were constructed by contract. It is well known that contractors deviate from specifications whenever and where ever it is possible to cut costs. It is entirely possible that at least some "off the shelf" computer chips have been used rather than the special designs that were specified. If those substitutions contain the same date problem as those purposefully in use for creating a chaotic breakdown of your world as you know it now, how will this affect their plans? Since there must be a synergistic exchange of information within computer systems there may well be repercussions within their own separately created system that will cause chaos within chaos. Portions of their plan may deploy, but in order to establish and then maintain complete control, which is their goal, all must proceed according to plan. What if enough of their plan moves into place for the people to realize the truth, but their own internal chaos allows for what we might call melt down from within? What if champions of mankind working within may have deliberately placed glitches within their systems? Interesting to contemplate.

Let us suppose that the above scenario is true. Now we have what might be called double chaos and exposure enough of the enslavement plan to bring humanity awake. This adds a 3rd layer of chaos. Out of all this chaos, how does the balance tip toward survival of humanity and the planet? There is one more element that must be interjected here. What of those extra-terrestrial beings that have been using the power structure they have coached into place? Would the above mentioned chaos serve their purposes? Could they have sabotaged the plans of their own henchmen in order to eliminate them from the game? Do they have in place a plan that overlays the ones that are in place? We might say that the plot thickens.

However, we could thicken it even more, since we are delving into possibilities. When one planet interferes with another to the detriment of the progress of that planet, we have the Universal Law of Attraction at work. Simply stated what you do unto another shall be done unto you. If you interfere with another planet, then you have given permission for other planetary forces to interact with you. Ah-ha! Does the thick plot begin to come into clarity? Let us hope that your heart just skipped a beat, and real hope has been born within your imagination.

We are still left with the dilemma of all that chaos. So, let us give a bit more clarity. Once a planet has been interfered with in a direct way, other than an advisory capacity, the inhabitants of that planet may *request* help in restoring balance and order. Herein lies the key. Help must be requested and prayer is considered requesting. However, it must be what is called affirmative prayer. Affirmative prayer is entering into the creative mode that is your pattern (made in the likeness and similitude of your Creator). Humanity must actually come forth in a group focus, in a harmonious creative mode within the upward spiral of the development of individual and planetary evolvement. Now, knowing human nature, there will be those who, when they have recovered from the shock, will immediately want to put back into place what is within their comfort zone. They will desire to take advantage of the situation to create another situation of power over the people, for indeed the cry will be for new "leaders". That would not be evolvement. The next level is based upon individual responsibility. Unless that is at the basis of the new paradigm the opportunity for the transcendence of this planet and its inhabitants will be lost.

What is important is that of an already perceived outline to be the "prayer of requesting help" needs to be in place to supersede any chances of returning to the old. The help you need to bring this into being will then be assured. This help will not be military in any way whatsoever. It will be the Love of the Creator manifested and shall be genuinely welcomed as it shall interact with the Inner Being that is the forgotten direct connection to the Creator. Love connecting and interacting with Love shall bring changes beyond your imagining abilities. It is also appropriate to note that on a planetary level, the planet itself shall have a like experience.

May this information offset your concerns about your futures! Welcome to the winning side! Focus and manifest, indeed!

No. 21

It is time to focus so that emphasis can be centered on the pivotal change necessary for the transition of the project from one phase to the next. This does not indicate that the first phase is already complete. That part, getting the information about the activities of the dark ones, is now in motion. From our point of view in watching energy composites, enough movement in the waking up phase is taking place to ensure its continuation. There are enough focused on getting the word out for it to continue within that momentum. Information is being discussed between people now, by those reading and hearing the information. As you know either by face to face discussion or through your computer Internet chat rooms, etc. the critical ripple effect is beginning. In order to keep the momentum, now that the wake up call is ringing, it is necessary to prepare the next step lest inertia caused by lack of understanding what to do next allows for the onslaught of mind numbing techniques to continue to hold the upper hand.

The next step is the choice of the individual to stand forth in determination to detach from the emotion of overwhelm and to observe from a space that is beyond the reach of the control techniques. It seems like a small step, but is critical for it is the beginning of the separation from the herd, so to speak. It is a step that can be accomplished without the danger that physical resistance would present. It is something that can be done in safety without being detected by the apparently fearsome entities that are striving for control. It is also critical in the process of each individual becoming aware that there is a connection to awareness, a part of self that allows for this observation. It triggers the shift within the over stimulated ego function and begins the calming of the ego. This will begin to bring it back into its true intended purpose. This in itself is an empowering experience, for it begins the balance of expression intended in the manifested experience. This is a very critical point. By establishing the observation experience, a change in focus begins to happen in a smooth and easy way.

How is it best to begin to fulfill your assignment? By purposefully practicing the process within yourself you will begin to guide those who are in contact with you that are waking to the knowledge of what is happening all around them. There is a fear element very active in their consideration of this information and how it appears it might affect their lives. It is not easy to contemplate all the marvelous conveniences disappearing from their experience and at the same time wondering how they will continue to make a living. It spells total poverty to them and so it is easier to keep shoving it to the back of their conscious awareness and not consider it. However, it continues to pop up into their thoughts like a bobber on a fishing line. It is appropriate then to suggest to them that they stand back from the problem and begin to consider what possibilities there are to use the situation to their advantage. Opportunities will present themselves through barter, trades and other methods yet to be created within the chaotic change period. Since it will be difficult to accumulate material wealth, this will free the creative aspect that is inherent in all fragments of the Creator. Creativeness is the keynote of experience at all levels, otherwise none of us would ever have been "thought" into existence. The key to all of this is asking for help from the focus of thought that brought forth this experience and holds us in it. If it were not for that focus the basic energy blocks (atoms, molecules and cells) would simply fly apart.

It seems difficult to correlate the probability of success for an entire planet, with only a few beginning a shift by simply changing their personal perspective and then encouraging a similar change in those in their sphere of influence. But that is how it is to be done. Just as a long journey begins with the first step, so also is change begun in individual experience. This is especially true when it follows the methodology that is the format for the operation of the Laws that govern manifested Creation. There must first exist something so that energy may be attracted to it. "In the beginning there was the 'thought', and the 'thought' became flesh (manifest)."

Following the conceptual thought, there must be the desire for it to manifest. To think the thought only does not bring it forth. There must be an emotional desire to provide the fuel for the movement or change of energy from thought into expression. Through coagulation of "attracted" energies, manifestation begins. Form includes more than things; it includes situations, circumstances and stimulation of desire for additional thoughts that support the completion of the desired experience. It is within the Creative impetus once the process is begun to move toward completion when the purpose is in harmony with the Universal Laws. The focus desired must provide freedom within the spiral journey of return to the Source for all that it will affect. When this is the underlying purpose then the Harmonic of Attraction is set in motion with all its subtle power released.

It is well to review the basics when a shift in creative focus is to begin in purposeful action of great magnitude. Each and every change in the destiny of this planet is received with great anticipation to the highest (finest vibratory) level of awareness. Those changes that will lead to the establishment of balance and harmony receive input of supporting energy that strengthens and hastens the process. It would be well to acknowledge this with gratitude as part of your meditations. The attitude of gratitude creates a return flow and allows for greater exchange of this supporting attentive awareness.

Beginning a change within a flow as firmly established as the planned hijacking of this planet, is the most difficult aspect of the project of returning this planet to the safety of harmony and balance. It has required considering responses to the recognition of distorted energies into action, and further to ferret out its source and its purpose. Then that understanding had to be put into written and spoken word and ways found to disseminate the information. All of this is to be accomplished within a flow of negative intention that not only is in motion, but also can be compared to a fast moving river. Yet you few are able to accomplish this seemingly impossible feat through intent fueled by desire to save your fellow beings and your planet from being exploited. Now, if we can continue the process with that same level of intent and desire to move many *through* the information about "them" to the next step, all shall continue toward the desired end result. Much of step one was accomplished without surface consciousness of where the knowledge and understanding of the situation engulfing humanity would lead. It was the need to inform and awaken so that "something" could be done. Thoughts of resistance through the original guidelines for continuing the government of the people fueled the process. Unfortunately government of the people by the people leads to tyranny in quick succession through many small steps.

Moving beyond into a new paradigm is the next step in the evolvement of the consciousness of humanity. Understanding that the ideal of freedom through personal responsibility offers the true solution is a big jump in perceived reality and would seem more so to the beginning few in accepting this theory as being possible and beginning to contemplate it. However, the impetus of the alternative of doing nothing during the collapse of the current experiment will supply pressure to consider new alternatives. The lack of a sense of personal responsibility within the ideal of elected governing entities will bring the realization of its importance as the key to success. The weakest link (muscle) must be strengthened by exercise. It must be given the opportunity of use in order to accomplish this strengthening. This must be the basis of the way out of the present situation to a new beginning.

Birthing this conception is next on the agenda. It will be like putting the second large rock into the flow of a fast river in order to divert it into another channel. Once the first rock is in place, then it is time to add the next one so that more water is diverted, however now there are more available to move that rock. There is a saying in your culture that in order to accomplish any difficult task it is the willing horse that must be whipped. It is not easy for the compassionate driver, but he knows that it is what must be done. Indeed, we bless you willing ones in these critical hours of this salvage operation. As you also say, "hang in there". It is indeed worth the effort.

No. 22

The failure of the planned conflagration is to be expected, for there must be a foe in order for that to happen. If indeed there are no armaments to oppose them, what will the dark forces do? There have been such conflicts, but the end result was not something to be repeated. There were self-appointed ones who knew of no other way to oppose distorted energy forces, and this resulted in two wrongs, which did not equate to a right. It is imperative that it be understood that armed resistance is futile. Those of us charged with assisting in resolving this situation will not support it. Though it has been mentioned before, it seemed appropriate to make this point entirely clear.

There is an interesting method of resistance employed by workers within industry when they are working in a factory situation in which the owners/managers are oppressive. It is called "malicious compliance". It is extremely effective over a period of time. In this instance, the employees do only that which they are told to do. They execute their assigned functions, but *nothing* else. For example, if a machine is breaking down, they do nothing about it. If an item of production is out of place as it moves down the line and will become entangled in any way, they do nothing. It was not in their job description. They cooperate in exactly the way they are told. Nothing is done to create a situation; they just allow the process to follow its natural course. Total compliance, no resistance and the situation deteriorates into chaos by its own momentum. An interesting course to contemplate.

Is this turning the other cheek? Not really! It is understanding the process of manifested creation outside of nature. That which comes into being through the focus of thought is maintained through continued focus. It continues as long as it serves its purpose and the focus of *positive* attention holds it in manifestation. When support for this is withdrawn, it returns to chaos. Management, as in the above example, rarely knows the exact functions and their focus is upon manipulating the workers, the customers and the balance sheet. There are too few holding the focus with positive intent for the manifestation to hold its form.

How then is nature different? Nature is Creation expressing in harmony with itself. Man did not create nature. Scientists are busy altering nature in your time. Ever bother to find out how long the hybrid distortions can be held in form? They cannot replicate themselves in perfection. The genes must be recombined, and often that does not happen according to past successes. It does happen when the intent is in harmony with Nature as in producing flowers of greater beauty and different colors. But the intent is to glorify, not exploit the process of nature. Most often, those who love the plant work *within the plant processes* to accomplish the successful changes.

The point of this discussion is to bring to your attention the importance of the intent of the group that desires to cooperate with Creation as they focus on the framework of the new paradigm. It is suggested that they consider nature as their ideal, this might give them a starting point. How indeed does nature fit into the whole of creation? How could humanity live in harmony with nature, rather than attempt to have dominion (power) over it? That does not mean that nature could not assist mankind in existing on this planet, but it should be a reciprocal relationship. The future would involve cooperating with nature within the Laws of the Universe.

But what are those laws? Where does humanity find those laws that have been hidden from them? In the small amount of time remaining, is there time to study nature and attempt to put together an accurate understanding that could be disseminated quickly enough? You must remember that what you need is available if you but ask. Already the Law of Attraction has been mentioned. But how many laws are there? Less than you might think. The number of applicable laws increases at each dimensional level, for the learning of these laws and their application allows for evolvement to the next level where there are more to learn and to apply within experience. Let us begin a review of these laws. It is a review because you have forgotten them in your sojourn to the 3rd dimensional experience.

The underlying Law of Creation is the Law of Attraction. Simply stated, like attracts like. It does this through the basic tool of Creation—*thought.* I believe your bible states "As a man thinketh, so is he." If you focus on the morass of evil once you are aware of it, you strengthen it. It is important to be aware of it, so that you may withdraw your support of it by using the second Law of Creation.

The Law of Deliberate Intent. Purposefully withdrawing your fear and fascination for the evil situation once you are aware of it, with the deliberate intent of doing so, is using this Law. You cannot do this by attempting to stop thinking about it. It is only possible to do this by substituting another thought on a completely different subject. In the case of the evil plan, it requires the total inclusion of those involved. It does not matter what the thoughts are as long as they support the plan. Complicity involves believing the intent of those involved is for the good of all. Perhaps now you can see the power of sympathy for the afflicted ones around your globe. This supports the victim consciousness that is required, for it is complicity in disguise. Do you not consider them victims of war or natural disaster or poverty? You must take a deep breath, accept your part in bringing support to their feelings of victimhood. They too have responsibility in the creation of those situations. Your sympathy will not solve their misery. Your deliberate choice to create a new paradigm of experience will do that. Withdrawing your focus of attention and bringing it toward creating a new experience will bring the change about far more quickly than repeatedly sending aid while considering them poor innocent victims. Does this sound hard hearted? From our point of view, it is hard hearted to be part of the creation of these horrendous situations in the first place. You must deliberately choose to implement your desire to create a whole new experience for them as well as yourselves. When you choose to place your intent beyond the play perceived by the 5 senses, and place it instead into the creation of a new experience, you are withdrawing your consent and support of the experience in which you no longer wish to participate. You are using the second Law of the Universe.

These are the two Laws that apply to this situation. There are yet two more and those shall be brought to bear within this information, as it is appropriate. It is important that we progress within the Laws, as they are applicable. It is important that you come to realize that the Laws of the Universe are immutable. They cannot be changed or distorted. They work without question as to who is applying them. When you consider the plan of evil intent that surrounds you, you can see them at work. Like attracts like and intent of purpose brings situations into being. However, we have attempted to bring to your understanding that there are nuances within these Laws that allow for Creation to continue. There needs to be an understanding and awareness of the leavening ingredient of Freewill followed by its proper use. Through this we have infinite variety within Creation and expansive movement results.

It is our hope that you will contemplate the implications of this information and that it will enlighten your understanding as well as strengthen your resolve to serve with our winning team.

No. 23

When we last had occasion to deal directly with those behind this plot, it was within a conference type situation. At that time, they were informed that there was full awareness of what their plan was set to accomplish. They were told that it was a futile attempt, but it was their choice to continue on in their chosen path. Inasmuch as freewill is the loose cannon of the Universal plan for evolvement, there was nothing we could do. Now it has reached the point at which their plan is indeed a threat, not that it could ever attain their desired goal of a negative universe/galaxy. It can however create unimaginable chaos. Do not take this information lightly. It is indeed a serious situation. This is not the fault of the inhabitants of Earth, it is just that this was the planet with the consciousness and physical manifested body type to fit the most ideal criteria for their plan. This is not the first time they have tried to overwhelm your planet to use it and humans for this purpose. It was a long time ago in your sequential counting. They were far advanced then in their technological gadgetry, but did not understand humanity, which allowed them to be repulsed. Unfortunately humanity chose to use force to do so and in that way buried within their psyche the belief that force was the way to solve any encroachment upon their perceived freedom. In a way, it married you to them through this perception.

This time, they believe that the earlier error in understanding their foe will not be repeated, for they have studied you well. Every weakness is known and is being exploited for their purposes. However, their focus was upon inducing your cooperation rather than resisting them until it is too late for you to do so. They carefully laid plans to overwhelm you both sensually and physically. In particular, they have emphasized safety over adventurous risk except within military paradigms. So you have insurance for all risky portions of your regimented life. You have your addictive paycheck system to depend upon, along with Social Security. (Notice it is always capitalized right along with your references to God. Even omnipresent Satan Claus is capitalized.) Your heroes are all well paid sports or movie stars. How adventurous are these? Your movie star heroes are drugged and adulterous in open display along with your presidential movie star. Remember, if you can be held at the lowest level of your dimension, you cannot take advantage of the dimensional leap at the shift of the cycles, but can instead be taken to an even lower level of vibration. At that point it is their intention to separate the soul energy from the body. They have no intention of putting it back into another body. It is the energy that they plan to use as power in the transformation of the chaos they intend to cause from positive to negative. They believe that the lower the vibration, the nearer it is to the still point, thus making it more malleable. All of these theories have been reached by attempting to study

Creation through the process of following its steps backward from manifestation to creative impetus.

Fortunately, there are many miscalculations in their plan. But not enough to avoid creating great chaos indeed if their plans progress much farther. Here again we are faced with the great stumbling block of freewill, the key ingredient in both bringing this situation into existence and causing it to self-destruct. This magical key is held by the consciousness of the beings on this planet. The consideration of the situation from the above point of view allows for it to seem to be a very bleak future indeed.

Enter the view from the other side, that of Creation. This view is adventurous, opportunistic and positive. It moves not upon long and exacting plans, but within a fluid and expansive mode. It moves within a creative stance that allows for enhancement of individual and collective experience rather than suppression and destruction. Remember the picture of the pond! The other side must control the ripples from the outside in, while WE may cause them great problems of containment by using just one small pebble, one idea continuing thought focused on creation. We have here two opposite modes of movement within the totality of Creation. Now, looking at the big picture, on which side would you place your bet?

It is not that our side does not have some problems to resolve, it is just that we have the innate natural expansive consciousness that harmonizes with the intended Life experience. Even though the conscious awareness appears to be mesmerized into sleep, how does one bring a hypnotized person back to consciousness? Is it not a snap of the fingers? But must that trigger be previously programmed? Not necessarily! Their planned trigger is the sudden mass realization of overwhelming control, an emotion they plan to feed upon with great enthusiasm. So, we have been busy triggering this realization in a slow and steady manner so as not to alert them to the damage that is being done to their planned trigger. Remember the 100th monkey theory? It is a slow and increasing dawning of understanding within the mass consciousness until a critical number reaches an awareness of a new concept and all know. Guess what! We are disarming their trigger. Are you aware of the awakening happening now? You were hoping for sudden realization while we were implementing the opposite. We are planning surprises of our own. It is indeed rewarding or fun as you put it, to be on the winning side and know it.

Now is the time to begin preparing the step in the process of a new focus for the awakening awareness of your planetary inhabitants. A new paradigm of experience! How fast must it move into the fray? Don't sweat that for a minute. Just do your part and all will come into play right on time. Once the first crack in their plan is complete, things will pick up in momentum. Just remember that we are hardly impotent. It is just that we must play the game according to the rules that insure success. Not so for our opponents! Keep in mind that the Creator must retain all of his fragments; even those that are our perceived opponents. He cannot stop caring for any part of the whole of His being.

*Note that we use the masculine within this information when referring to the Creator. It is just that creating is an attribute of the masculine focus, while the womb or ability to contain the creation of the masculine function is considered the feminine attribute. Through this we have the depiction of the masculine Creator and the mother Earth. Indeed it is balanced in wholeness of experience. We would prefer that the women of Earth would come into this understanding and find their balance within it soon.

May these glimmers of understanding be blessings indeed, as

you continue to fulfill your commitments within this wondrous event. Keep on keeping on!

No. 24

It is within the scope of the information to bring through the basic framework of the underlying movement of how we may assist you to spearhead the ripples of change that will spread outward through the mass consciousness. Remember that when the pebble is first cast, the first outward ripples would seem quite inconsequential, but in the moments that follow, they move outward in ever widening circles. This process works when the waters of the pond are still. The mass consciousness is indeed mesmerized into stillness through the methodology employed by the planners of this situation. That does not include ones involved in skirmishes of war, but when the totality of the billions of beings upon the planet is considered you must remember there are many who are not reached by the media communications and are unaware of any of this drama. Therefore the surface of the mass conscious awareness remains quite still. This is the reason that it is imperative that we accomplish our goals to interject our changes within the individual awareness of key individuals now. It is the slow and undetectable change of thought patterns within each individual that comes into contact with this knowledge, that is the underlying foundation of our building process. The talk radio programs as well as the supporting data available on the Internet are making an impact with additional printed and visual material for those who have yet to understand and process the wake up information more completely.

This format is reaching countless individuals who have this within their conscious and sub-conscious levels of mind. Their degree of denial on the conscious level does not matter at this moment in the sequence of events. The information is there to be remembered when some item of news or event in their experience will trigger the remembering of it. The Internet reaches around the planet and the mushrooming of interest in available information is a measure of the thirst for this knowledge and is a small indication of what is going on. Please note that had one of the talk show hosts indeed stopped his involvement, there was backup present and already in operation. Volunteers are given opportunity, but backups are standing by not only waiting, but already in position. Ours is not a slap-dash poorly planned operation. Just as the opposition has focused energy to lay their plans and to implement them; this was not unknown to us. In the observation of these, there were plans in readiness so that any possibility to end their endeavor at earlier stages was possible. Indeed, a chess game of great magnitude has been in progress for a very long time in your counting. Now we are down to the final moves.

The understanding of this basic framework of the plan involves seeing your part in the initiation of this phase as being within the first pebble. To bring change to a mass consciousness involving billions of individual points of awareness by a small group of focused group awareness is indeed a tiny pebble. It is the focused aspect that makes the difference, especially when that focus is in harmony with the underlying purpose of the Creator. As that focus encompasses a larger and larger group, the pebble becomes larger and larger. Just because it has reached the surface of the pond of mass consciousness of those inhabitants of the planet, it has not yet reached the level of the surface of the pond of awareness of the planet Herself.

The level of awareness of Earth consciousness is a whole new ball game, which has never been explored by the humanity in this sojourn you refer to as the current wave of planetary civilization. It was known and understood at what might be called "priestly" levels long ago, but the information was not disseminated. Just as there are what you call beings of awareness that have transcended 3rd dimensional experience and who are devoted to the task of assisting you in this process, so also are there foci of awareness that serve in that purpose at the planetary level. Those are fully aware of this situation and have not yet brought their influence to bear. What you perceive as influences involving Earth herself, are as yet just normal reactions to distorted patterns brought forth by the extreme misuse of your home base. If the action within the mass consciousness does not bring about the desired changes, then a pebble of different origin will ripple that conscious pond and indeed there shall be movement on that level which will not be kind to the inhabitants. Unfortunately that level of awareness is oblivious to individual humans and so all shall experience and survive, or not, those events by their own intuition as to placement and movements within the events as they occur. It is still possible to bring about the reversal of planned misuse of the inhabitants and the planet without that level of involvement.

As you can see by following the messages, there are multiple levels of involvement in this situation, and we have but barely scratched the surface. It is not planned to overwhelm you with information, but only to bring forth that which will serve your understanding that you are not abandoned, but are supported fully so that the opportunity to transcend through the cycles may be fully available. It is not necessary that all of humanity be given this information in order for them to participate at this moment in your timing. Most would not even consider it. It is for those that are open to it and find comfort in knowing that their efforts are acknowledged and supported. Most have moved on with their assignments without knowing why or how to accomplish them, but have taken advantage of opportunity and kept going because there was a knowingness that it was what they "had" to do. That is courage indeed, which does not go unrecognized in the final accounting of this endeavor.

Blessings to all that read and consider this information, for it is given in the focus of Love within that which is the Source of this opportunity through experience.

No. 25

Now that we are beginning to reach a level of understanding of the basic format that is the foundation for your cooperative focus within the larger view, it is possible to expand into more levels of information. These are not at the physical activity level, but in the more important area of using creative thought. Inasmuch as you are a focused fragment of the Creator's aware-ness, it is now time for you to begin to fulfill your purpose of expanding the use of the holographic concept that has been the vehicle of your trip into 3rd dimensional experience.

This is not a process intended to overwhelm or cause resis-tance within your awareness. These concepts are known to you at deeper levels, and will seem quite familiar provided you relax and follow the wording. These will begin to stir the inner remem-brance process. It is within your understanding that a fragment of a whole can through the holographic process depict the whole. It is through the projection of light through the fragment that the illusion of the whole from which it came is reproduced so that the nature of the whole can be known. If this is the case, then you are a picture of the Whole from which you were projected. If this is true, then how can there be diversity in what is seen all around you? Shouldn't this be a world of exact replicas? If the Source of the replicated whole were limited to one focus of experience, then that would be true.

However, if the Whole of that Source is multi-dimensional and within its makeup holds the potentiality of multiple foci of purpose, then each projected fragment draws upon that unlimited field of possibilities. Thought provides the mobility that allows Creation to flow into manifestation. Thought has the potential of thinking within and upon itself. This is another way of describing Freewill. Thus these added levels of activity enable endless variety to be present.

Now if that is true, why then isn't every fragment *totally* different? You were created in the image and similitude of that which projected you into existence. Here the law of attraction of similar yet different is seen at work. If that was absent, then there could be no exchange of thought and Creation would be just an unending field of unrelated diversity. Enter what you call intelligence, which is nothing more than thought thinking within itself and observing itself observe itself, a spiraling activity. Focused thought thinks itself outward into manifestation. This is a slowing of the vibratory rate of the extended thought to the lowest level at which it can contain its purposeful intent. At that point the manifested thought can no longer perceive its Source. It is in a state of thinking awareness that can now perceive itself and its surrounding environment. In your vernacular, it can no longer clearly remember the nature of its Source, so it has forgotten. Since it is projected thought, it must maintain its connection in order to remain in manifestation. Through this connection, lies the potentiality of the fragment focusing its own thought processes purposefully back through this connective energy flow and then beginning to "remember" what it is, which is again thought thinking within and upon itself.

Since the holographic projection is an extension process of outward movement of thought, the natural inclination is to continue the outward movement through the use, in this scenario, of its sensatory tools to think (observe). Indeed we could go on for volumes of books to cover the beginning story of this planet and its history of inhabitants, but that would take us far afield from the purpose of this message. The point is to help you realize that thought thinking within and upon itself is commonly experienced by you because it is exactly what you are. Through choice you create diverse experiences. Through thinking and choosing, each experiences commonly shared situations differently. This is the natural flow of Creation within Itself.

This sounds idealistic when the current situation surrounding you is considered. When multiple human beings (extensions of thought from higher dimensional foci) experience interactions, combined thought patterns evolve. These thought patterns in movement are something like your breathing process. They expand to a certain point and then relax and contract by returning first to a restive state. Involved within this process you experience positive and negative polarities, or so you have named them. It is a slow spiraling process, just as your breathing process was intended to assist you in a slow spiraling process.

If these are the parameters of experience, then you can begin to perceive that the contraction-relaxation phase of your process in this moment of planetary experience is not in a normal state. It is very distorted indeed. Your intended freedom of thought choice process has been violated. It is layers of thought distortion experiencing contraction that has bypassed the restive point that normally allows for the return to the expansive mode. Hopefully you can now overlay this understanding upon the planetary experience. If so, you see that in order for the distorted plan to accomplish their moment of beginning, following use of planned chaos, which is to be their field of opportunity to cause a change of polarity, they must allow the restive point to be reached. Their ideal is to attain this by overwhelming the greater part of the conscious awareness of this planet through a majority of its inhabitants. This is to be teamed with the ending, or shifting of a major Creative cycle in this Galaxy. There exists within their timing and their methodology their greatest weakness. For the contraction of awareness beyond the Universal norm, when placed in a momentary rest point, sets up the opportunity for a reactive expansion of major proportions. Carefully placed triggers within the same contracted awareness can ensure this expansion. Welcome to the winning side! Focus and manifest! Indeed!

No. 26

It is now appropriate through the shift of greater understanding within the key group of visionaries to begin the focus of the conception of the new paradigm of experience. As is the pattern, many will receive this cosmic stimulation, and the perfect few will respond when the opportunity to participate is presented. Keep in mind that this continuing process will move through phases of birthing within the awareness individually and collectively in a subtle calm transcending movement. Do not expect a massive jumping on the bandwagon type of reaction. It will move outward in a whisper of awareness. Again, think in terms of the patterns of nature. When you observe nature you see spirals in the slow process of growth as in the spiral of shell formation and within the functioning of breathing. Though invisible in form, it is the process that begins at birth and carries each mammalian form through its sequential life. Consider the birthing process through the format of breathing, expansion and contraction causing movement toward the goal within a transcending spiral and carrying it to completion. You will see a traveling outward of conceptual information, an inbreath of consideration, again a traveling outward and an inbreath of shared discussion, moving toward the desired focus of new experience. The intent fueled by the desire for new experience will bring forth the process which is being built upon the foundation of foci provided by multiple levels of awareness with supporting intent for this situation to move into a new paradigm.

This is the appropriate moment to consider a self-defeating concept that needs to be corrected to insure success. Through long planted misinformation by the religions on your planet, you think of the focused assistance as coming to you from the outside. You look outward at the surrounding lights in your sky at night and presume it is coming from "out there." Indeed, it is possible to exchange energies at the level of manifestation, however the flow of Creation is from the inside out. It is an expansive process. Again we must remind you of the in and out flow of the breathing process. What your scientists observe as burn out and destruction through black holes, etc. is instead evidence of the breathing process incorporating the spiraling changes of shifts into higher vibratory dimensions. As this happens, *appropriate* energy fields move through this process. If it was all energy, then what is observed would long ago have been "devoured" by one single black hole. (Here again you can begin to understand the magnitude of the plans of the negative focus in attempting to create through the process of pushing this Galaxy through a process opposite the creative flow into an opposing reality.) What is perceived by the scientists as the compaction of energy into a tiny ball of massive molecular weight, is of course, total nonsense. The energy is expanding within the conversion process by increasing its vibrational levels as it moves into a new paradigm of expression. Is this Galaxy, or a small portion of it going through the black hole process? There is no awareness of it. What if it was true? If it were to happen, it would hardly be a hellacious experience.

Let us return to the point. To say that our plan is in motion does not mean that conscious contacts with seemingly appropriate beings of shared purpose and dedication are near completion. It is this process of conception that is the focus of these lessons. That which is to be accomplished at more subtle levels depends upon this process proceeding within defined parameters. The outflow of this information to those of commitment is encouraged. It is most meaningful in the whole of it, but each can stand alone as is appropriate. Key words to trip the intercept triggers have been for the most part avoided and the references to beings and processes of "interest" are made as subtly as possible. It is time that the usage of those be virtually eliminated as our focus of intent is on information that educates and informs you of the true nature of yourselves and the energetic forms and functions of the Creation of which you are an intregal part.

Let us make a point clear. This focus of information is not "God" speaking directly to you. That which you call by that name is a confused and misunderstood scramble of misinformation. What has happened is that what could be personified into the Creator of this Galaxy is not the focus of the whole of All That Is. To make this understandable, perhaps, let us return again to the breathing process as an example. The underlying All That Is is pure potentiality and even finer levels beyond that which are imperceptible because to perceive would be to limit it. At its conceptual level, breathing is expansion as you breathe out, rest, in breathe, rest and repeat. Potentiality is most available for "absorption" (big generalization) in the moments of rest. Throughout the entirety of the expression of Potentiality into experience are varying degrees of awareness that have begun their return trips by first realizing they are holographic tiny fragments of the focus of their Creator. This creative focus is in turn a tiny fragment of a finer more encompassing focus of the Potentiality that underlies a greater Creation that has at some point been birthed from that which lies beyond in an unknowable state. Will we return to that state of unknowingness? Is that our goal at the farthermost reaches of eternity? Doubt it, for it appears that in order to move through the return trip, just exactly the opposite is necessary in order to progress. You must remember that one of your greatest distortions in understanding Creation at this level is your concept of needing to measure experience as linear, in what you call time. It is also a great barrier for those of us who are too interested in experience to bother to measure it. We can conceive of no reason to do so, for we know Divine Order has no sequential parameters.

As we return to our discussion of your concept of "God" you can now see why we have substituted the term "Creation" and "Creator" instead of using "God," in the hope that we could begin to change your perception. The word "God" itself conjures up feelings that cause inner turmoil in many, since at a deeper level they know that the religious teachings through a long sequence of experience have brought them only confusion. These have given them a distorted representation of the Source of their origin. It is important that those who intend to bring forth the new paradigm have at least a basic clarity as to the nature of their identity and of the Source of their existence. What lies beyond this Galaxy is, at this moment, outside the necessity to understand. To know that it *IS*, is all that is necessary. Our focus lies within the Creation of our Creator. He (androgynous but in the masculine creative mode) can be called "God", but frankly a new name is recommended. You may address communication to Him, but it is only received when it harmonizes with the creative outflow of His expression. "In His Name" as an expression in your bible was meant to tell you to place your focus of prayer within that purposeful intention. You are to make a request that intends creation, within the harmony of His attitude of "all that is necessary to bring what you desire is available for your use. You are a fragment of Him and through you, He (the "I am" awareness of your connection) is experiencing expansion of the total awareness that is You/He." As you do this, it is a shared experience. As a fragment of Him, you create by attraction all your experiences. But, using the Law of Intention in harmonious cooperation within His expansive mode is how you create purposeful or *new* paradigms of experience.

It is hoped this information is a blessing through the expansion of your understanding of who and what you are! Yours is a glorious heritage, celebrate it!

No. 27

When your perception of time is adjusted to include the possibility of giving up as unimportant, the necessity of measuring experience in blocks, rather than allowing it to simply flow through your experience you will have surpassed a great impediment to your progress. Earlier in the existence of your planet, there was not a tilt in the axis and so the seasons as you know them did not exist. This confined plant and animal existence to the more moderate temperature zones, but the growth was more prolific and extended further into the colder areas than you might think because of adaptation. The effect of the tilt caused you to have the seasons as one more block of experience to measure as time.

A continuum of days and nights within an unchanging overall weather pattern brings a more relaxed focus on the necessity to measure time within survival experience. Before the distortion of the energy of competition, cooperation was one key to existence. When the lifestyles of what you refer to as indigenous tribes in the equatorial latitudes of your planet are considered, there is much less emphasis on measuring blocks of time and more cooperation within the survival groups. There is less competition between groups than is depicted in your movies, excluding areas like Africa because of planned outside influences. These are considerations to be included within your new paradigm. The greater the unbalance of the planetary inhabitants, the greater the imbalance of the planet as a whole. Within the changing of the galactic cycles lies the opportunity for re-balancing both the inhabitants and the planet. This does not mean that the planet would necessarily move 23 degrees back to perfect balance, but indeed some change could be made.

It is interesting to note that there is a move among what you refer to as "liberal political views" toward the elimination of competition within the educational experiences of your children and it is being met with stiff resistance. Of course there are ulterior motives for this would further calm the children into less and less creative modes of experience. Athletic competitions bring forth desires to excel and the concept transfers over into desire to excel in other areas. This has been a larger stumbling block for their plans than was anticipated. As an interesting side note, the greatest improvements in lifestyle, art and genuine music happen during lengthy periods of peace when there is no competition within warring conflicts. The history of China has long periods of freedom from being overrun by other cultural groups and little intermarriage with outside groups. Unfortunately over population was a counter-balance and these improvements were not widely available to all the citizens. Nonetheless, the focus was turned inward toward contemplation and desire for greater experience of uplifting and more joyful existence. Much was accomplished during those periods.

The new paradigm must include within it the desire to lift the human experience above the pivotal thought and behavior patterns that force distortions to be repeated generation after generation. The desire to do this is apparent in the myriad self-help books, tapes and well-trodden paths to the psychologist and psychiatrist offices. The approach is from the outside inward by considering the action and attempting to find the buried experience that has caused the reactive habits. Here again envisioning a new paradigm and focusing on experiencing this instead of fixing the old would empower the desired new realm of existence. However, even if accomplished, the ability to maintain a different level of experiencing within the surrounding environment would be difficult indeed. As more than one crab in a basket will not allow any to escape from the basket, so it is with human experience. The new paradigm must be a cooperative group focus of desire within a clearly stated purpose that can be held in focus for a period long enough to bring it into manifestation.

You can now understand that what the focus group must accomplish is to create a clearly stated purpose that is appealing to all of humanity. Attached is the apologia of an essay written in 1899, long before instant communication. It chronicles what happened when it was published in a small inconsequential magazine.

It was called "A Message to Garcia". If this one inspirational message could travel the globe then think what effect one encompassing message of purpose could do within our goal! Though the focus of getting the information out about the existence of the evil planners and of their deeds as far as you have been able to discover them is indeed the necessary first step, it has not rallied a reactive response. It is just as well for as we have said before, the victim/martyrdom which it might have engendered are not part of the true paradigm of experience within the Creative flow. What is needed is a pivot point that can be accomplished before the closing of the cycles. It need not be accomplished in a simultaneous moment. It is best as an event within each individual's conscious awareness. That process does not make it less of a pivot point. It would lay the groundwork for the greater pivotal changes in conscious awareness that *will* happen within sequential experience.

Again we remind you that freewill allows those who choose to remain in the pattern of present existence. *Do not be concerned with those.* The ingredient of freewill in the soup of experience teaches us another of the Universal Laws, that of Allowance. Personal responsibility is just that—PERSONAL. It means that one is concerned with the choosing of his/her own experience and is not responsible for the experience of others. All are allowed to participate within a group focus of cooperative experience or not. However choosing not to participate does have its consequences. Those who choose deliberately to withhold their participation in ending the present paradigm will be allowed to continue it elsewhere in a somewhat different format. They are *allowed* to choose their mode of experience in this situation. Allowance is the most difficult of the laws to be learned at the 3rd dimensional level because of the deeply ingrained need to control. Control is transcended through the practice of the Law of

Allowance. At this point in this discussion, we encounter the situation of child abuse. Children are within the influence of their parents' belief systems. What the parents believe and focus upon draw experiences to the family group. Information of past family history is encoded within the combination of genes which accounts for events happening to some members of a family and not to others. It emphasizes the fact that parenting involves more than *dealing* with planned or unplanned children. It is the personal responsibility of each parent and both parents together to raise the children within an understanding of the wide scope of influences such an undertaking involves.

It is important at this point to discuss the capitalization of various words in this text. It is intended that this material be as free of *religious* connotations as possible. Current and past experiences with priestly manipulation and control cause immediate shut down or distortion of understanding information that contains these references because of the misinformation about the control of what you call god. We can assure you that the creator could care less if you honor him by capitalizing all references to him. He is much more interested in whether or not you harmonize within the outflow of his creative focus. There is a problem because the very words you choose to indicate awareness of this flow of energy engender reactive feelings. This cannot be helped, so it is best to at least do away with all the capitals. It is one trigger that is best left inactive.

It is our intent that this continuing discussion brings a deepening understanding with regard to the purpose that looms in your immediate future. It is hoped that it strengthens and supports your commitment to continue on with your progress along the path of completion of this segment of experience. However, don't plan on long R & R leaves at its ending.

A Message to Garcia
by Elbert Hubbard
(Fra Elbertus)

The Roycrofters
East · Avrora · Erie · Covray · NY

Apologia

This literary trifle, *A Message to Garcia*, was written one evening after supper, in a single hour. It was on the Twenty-second of February, Eighteen Hundred Ninety-nine, Washington's Birthday, and we were just going to press with the March *Philistine*. The thing leaped hot from my heart, written after a trying day, when I had been endeavoring to train some rather delinquent villagers to abjure the comatose state and get radioactive.

The immediate suggestion, though, came from a little argument over the teacups, when my boy Bert suggested that Rowan was the real hero of the Cuban War. Rowan had gone alone and done the thing—carried the message to Garcia.

It came to me like a flash! Yes, the boy is right, the hero is the man who does his work—who carries the message to Garcia.

I got up from the table, and wrote *A Message to Garcia*. I thought so little of it that we ran it in the Magazine without a heading. The edition went out, and soon orders began to come for extra copies of the March *Philistine*, a dozen, fifty, a hundred;

and when the American News Company ordered a thousand, I asked one of my helpers which article it was that had stirred up the cosmic dust. "It's the stuff about Garcia," he said.

The next day a telegram came from George H. Daniels, of the New York Central Railroad, thus: "Give price on one hundred thousand Rowan articles in pamphlet form — Empire State Express advertisement on back — also how soon can ship."

I replied giving price, and stated we could supply the pamphlets in two years. Our facilities were small and a hundred thousand booklets looked like an awful undertaking.

The result was that I gave Mr. Daniels permission to reprint the article in his own way. He issued it in booklet form in editions of half a million. Two or three of these half-million lots were sent out by Mr. Daniels, and in addition the article was reprinted in over two hundred magazines and newspapers. It has been translated into all written languages.

At the time Mr. Daniels was distributing the *Message to Garcia*, Prince Hilakoff, Director of the Russian Railways, was in this country. He was the guest of the New York Central, and made a tour of the country under the personal direction of Mr. Daniels. The prince saw the little book and was interested in it, more because Mr. Daniels was putting it out in such big numbers, probably, than otherwise.

In any event, when he got home he had the matter translated into Russian, and a copy of the booklet given to every railroad employee in Russia.

Other countries then took it up, and from Russia it passed into Germany, France, Spain, Turkey, Hindustan, and China. During the war between Russia and Japan, every Russian soldier who went to the front was given a copy of the *Message to Garcia*.

The Japanese, finding the booklets in possession of the

Russian prisoners, concluded that it must be a good thing, and accordingly translated it into Japanese. And on an order of the Mikado, a copy was given to every man in the employ of the Japanese Government, soldier or civilian. Over forty million copies of *A Message to Garcia* have been printed. This is said to be a larger circulation than any other literary venture of the author, in all history — thanks to a series of lucky accidents!

E.H.
East Aurora,
December 1, 1913

"A Message to Garcia"

In all this Cuban business there is one man that stands out on the horizon of my memory like Mars at perihelion.

When war broke out between Spain and the United States, it was very necessary to communicate quickly with the leader of the Insurgents. Garcia was somewhere in the mountain fastnesses of Cuba—no one knew where. No mail or telegraph message could reach him. The President must secure his cooperation, and quickly. What to do!

Someone said to the President, "There is a fellow by the name of Rowan who will find Garcia for you, if anybody can."

Rowan was sent for and given a letter to be delivered to Garcia. How the "fellow by the name of Rowan" took the letter, sealed it up in an oilskin pouch, strapped it over his heart, in four days landed by night off the coast of Cuba from an open boat, disappeared into the jungle, and in three weeks came out on the other side of the Island, having traversed a hostile country on foot, and delivered his letter to Garcia — are things I have no special desire now to tell in detail. The point that I wish to make is this: McKinley gave Rowan a letter to be delivered to Garcia; Rowan took the letter and did not ask, "Where is he at?"

By the Eternal there is a man whose form should be cast in deathless bronze and the statue placed in every college of the land. It is not book-learning young men need, nor instruction about this and that, but a stiffening of the vertebrae which will cause them to be loyal to a trust, to act promptly, concentrate their energies: do the thing — "Carry a message to Garcia."

General Garcia is dead now, but there are other Garcias. No man who has endeavored to carry out an enterprise where many hands were needed, but has been well-nigh appalled at times by the imbecility of the average man—the inability or unwillingness to concentrate on a thing and do it.

Slipshod assistance, foolish inattention, dowdy indifference, and half-hearted work seem the rule; and no man succeeds, unless by hook or crook or threat he forces or bribes other men to assist him; or mayhap, God in His goodness performs a miracle, and sends him an Angel of Light for an assistant.

You, reader, put this matter to a test: You are sitting now in your office — six clerks are within call. Summon any one and make this request: "Please look in the encyclopedia and make a brief memorandum for me concerning the life of Corregio," Will the clerk quietly say, "Yes, sir," and go do the task?

On your life he will not. He will look at you out of a fishey eye and ask one or more of the following questions: Who was he? Which encyclopedia? Was I hired for that? Don't you mean Bismark? What's the matter with Charlie doing it? Is he dead? Is there any hurry? Shan't I bring you the book and let you look it up yourself? What do you want to know for? And I will lay you ten to one that after you have answered the questions, and explained how to find the information, and why you want it, the clerk will go off and get one of the other clerks to help him try to find Garcia — and then come back and tell you there is no such man. Of course, I may lose my bet, but according to the Law of Average, I will not. Now, if you are wise, you will not bother to explain to your "assistant" that Correggio is indexed under the C's, not in the K's, but you will smile very sweetly and say, "Never mind," and go look it up yourself. And this incapacity for independent action, this oral stupidity, this infirmity of the will, this unwillingness to cheerfully catch hold and lift — these are the things that put pure Socialism so far into the future. If men will not act for themselves, what will they do when the benefit of their effort is for all?

A first mate with knotted club seems necessary; and the dread of getting "the bounce" Saturday night holds many a worker to his place. Advertise for a stenographer, and nine out of ten who apply can neither spell nor punctuate — and do not think it necessary to.

Can such a one write a letter to Garcia? "You see that bookkeeper," said the foreman to me in a large factory. "Yes; what about him?"

"Well, he's a fine accountant, but if I'd send him uptown on an errand, he might accomplish the errand, and on the other hand, might stop at four saloons on the way, and when he got to Main Street would forget what he had been sent for." Can such a man be entrusted to carry a message to Garcia?

We have recently been hearing much maudlin sympathy expressed for the "down-trodden denizens of the sweatshop" and the "homeless wanderer searching for honest employment," and with it all often go many hard words for the men in power.

Nothing is said about the employer who grows old before his time in a vain attempt to get frowsy ne'er-do-well to do intelligent work; and his long, patient striving after "help" that does nothing but loaf when his back is turned. In every store and factory there is a constant weeding-out process going on. The employer is constantly sending away "help" that have shown their incapacity to further the interests of the business, and others are being taken on. No matter how good times are, this sorting continues: only, if times are hard and work is scarce, the sorting is done finer — but out and forever out the incompetent and unworthy go. It is the survival of the fittest. Self-interest prompts every employer to keep the best of those who can carry a message to Garcia.

I know one man of really brilliant parts who has not the ability to manage a business of his own, and yet who is absolutely worthless to anyone else, because he carries with him constantly the insane suspicion that his employer is oppressing, or intending to oppress him. He can not give orders, and he will not receive them. Should a message be given him to take to Garcia, his answer would probably be, "Take it yourself!" Tonight this man walks the streets looking for work, the wind whistling through his threadbare coat. No one who knows him dare employ him, for he is a regular firebrand of discontent. He is impervious to reason, and the only thing that can impress him is the toe of a thick-soled Number Nine boot.

Of course I know that one so morally deformed is no less to be pitied than a physical cripple; but in our pitying let us drop a tear, too, for the men who are striving to carry on a great enterprise, whose working hours are not limited by whistle, and whose hair is fast turning white through the struggle to hold in line dowdy indifference, slipshod imbecility, and the heartless ingrat-

FOR THE NEW PARADIGM

itude which, but for their enterprise, would be both hungry and homeless.

Have I put the matter too strongly? Possibly I have; but when all the world has gone a-slumming I wish to speak a word of sympathy for the man who succeeds — the man who, against great odds, has directed the efforts of others, and having succeeded, finds there's nothing in it: nothing but bare board and clothes. I have carried a dinner-pail and worked for day's wages, and have also been an employer of labor, and I know there is something to be said on both sides. There is no excellence, per se, in poverty: rags are no recommendation; and all employers are not rapacious and highhanded, any more than all poor men are virtuous. My heart goes out to the man who does his work when the "boss" is away, as well as when he is at home. And the man who, when given a letter for Garcia, quietly takes the missive, without asking any idiotic questions, and with no lurking intention of chucking it into the nearest sewer, or of doing aught else but deliver it, never gets "laid off," nor has to go on a strike for higher wages. Civilization is one long, anxious search for just such individuals. Anything such a man asks shall be granted. He is wanted in every city, town and village — in every office, shop, store and factory. The world cries out for such: he is needed and needed badly — the man who can "Carry a Message to Garcia."

No. 28

As your need to experience in calculated time passes into relative unimportance, the momentum of your experiences of the new paradigm will flow smoothly into a release of the materialistic mode that holds you tightly within the power of the deviant perpetrators. It is the pursuit of the creation of your personal fiefdoms and the competition to create one of greater opulence and grander physical pleasures that have you trapped. These are empty promises to fill the void of imbalance that you feel within. Subliminal messages are planted within all the advertisement to feed your materialistic addictions. The tangled and layered morass of information and lies is reminiscent of the fable of the lion and the mouse. The lion of humanity lies staked to the earth, held fast by the net of distraction of the conscious mind. In the story it took a tiny mouse to chew through the ropes to release the lion. In our version of the story, it is the radio talk show, the available Internet information and the publication of books and tapes that constitute the mouse. The information shared is based on personal experience and researches of archives of information available to any that care to take advantage of it. The integrity of the net is threatening to give way. Once released, the lion is then aware of the power of the tiny mouse so anything could happen. Unfortunately, there are more nets in place unless we take charge of the story line and change the scenario.

The point of these messages is to encourage and to inform, not educate in the format as it is practiced. There are no subliminal subversive intentions hidden within them. Each of you has programmed within the deep levels of your awareness the memory of the purpose you came into this lifetime to accomplish. We are simply keeping our agreement to remind you and to give guidance and direction to your actions. When the focus is on reacting to what is perceived as eminent danger, then momentum is lost. It is our agreed function to share the view that we are privileged to have from a dimension encompassing a greater vision of the situation. We view energy patterns in movement in a holographic display, and can model the various possibilities available. This is an advantage. It is the purpose of this information to share what is allowed within the universal laws governing freewill with as much clarity as possible. We find allegorical stories are remembered and applied to overall understanding most effectively. We are limited to those available through the experiences of the translator of this information. It is a dictation/translation/transcription process with the translation portion being the most critical component. It is important that this person continue to input information to enhance the available "database". Guidance is provided to appropriate materials.

It is within the allowable guidelines to bring to your attention deviations within those patterns that can be corrected because it is your freewill decision whether or not to do so. The problem of getting the information to you is massive indeed. Face to face discussions are not possible for many reasons but mostly because victim/martyrdom is not in our experience pattern and that would be the end result. Therefore we have this process as a more effective way. Though there is no 2-way exchange possible at this time and it is not necessary.

It is also possible for us to bring much information into the awareness of those committed to the project. Through the acceptance of this commission and a commitment to participate and see it through, the energy matrix of each changes and this is observed. This opens a line of communication and also results in a change of activity within the inner dimensional (sleep) states.

These changes are reflected in the outer dimensional activities during the day. Many changes in these lives will be noted, from the mundane to major shifts in attitudes and choices of activities. As mental and physical activities change, the intent and commitment become more focused and a spiral effect begins to occur within the levels of consciousness. You *are* being supported in this process!

It is with trepidation that we bring to your attention that the open communication lines are now under greater control and it is their intention to identify those yet unknown individuals who disseminate information that counters their plans. As yet it is in the identification process and has not moved beyond into retribution. This is because there are purposes for allowing you the privilege to do what you are doing that are not known to all levels of oppression. The word identification process is being further expanded. We suggest strongly that you edit your verbal and written conversations. Book wording can be read electronically, but titles especially are being processed. If suspicious, then the forward/epilogue portions are to be reviewed. Expect bookstore chains to be contacted and told to remove titles from the shelves and raids to take place at wholesale/distributor levels as the next step. Hopefully they will be discriminating and take only certain individual items, however that has not been the pattern. This will limit your freedom to print and distribute freely, so creativity must be used in the wording of titles, forwards and endorsement information. It suggests the possibility of setting up alternate locations and different names with books, etc. likely to pass through the first two tests. This might be considered as possible joint efforts if the hurdle of profit sharing can be worked *through*. If reprints are being considered, or new books or tapes, these considerations may be important. Creativity in promotional copy will be challenging. Intuitive inspiration is available on request. Smile! You *are on* the winning side!

No. 29

It is with *resolve* that you must *focus* the energy of intent into bringing forth this phase of the project. There is indeed a nuance of difference in these. One can intend to do something but never actually do it. Resolve is the spark that holds the intent in the forefront of the field of activity within your awareness. "This phase" refers to what might be called the second layer of activity toward initiation of the project. The phase of "getting the word out" does not cease because a new phase has begun. One simply adds the beginning of the next phase in a layering sense. Phase one was something like the foundation of a pyramid. Now we are beginning the second layer of the construction before the first layer is complete. Visualize how graphics complete a picture on the computer. It begins and does not always complete the picture in totally horizontal motion one line at a time and the picture is at some point complete. Next, consider this in a holographic focus for the planet. In your mind's eye, you can see where the information has gone and "paint" in areas where your information has been sent. If you see the planet as dark and the information painted in as lighted areas you can begin to "get the picture". You could see the sprinkles of light spread outward.

Even people who have heard and consciously rejected the information reflect a degree of light and it remains waiting to fully reflect. It is because you cannot know how many of these there are that you have difficulty in grasping the magnitude of accomplishment that this phase has reached and it continues to expand. The 100th monkey point is very close indeed. Portions of phase two are already in motion and momentum will expand it much more quickly than phase one. Because of the awareness brought forth by phase one, there are many that are waiting and wondering what it is that they can do, now that they are aware. We shall provide that answer and it will seem to them an easy thing to do, for they are being asked to do something that can be done privately and without drawing any notice. *And* it is the most powerful thing that needs to be done. It is a focused pivotal change of attitude from victim to empowerment.

The great resistance to phase one information was because each thought it would involve armed revolution to accomplish *change.* We know that a change is not our goal. A new paradigm of experience begins with totally different techniques and methods and there is no counter measure in place once it is begun. It can be countered only with reactive measures that would be deviations within the negative plan. This would bring forth chaos within that focus. The negative plan is counter to the flow of creative energy within which it exists. It requires continuity and narrowly defined focus that links together. This is absolutely essential.

It is with joy that we share these segments of information so that you may begin to understand more than just the nature of the negative plans, but also to understand the weak links available within their plan are opportunities. We can continue to guide you as to how to "gnaw away" at those links as long *as we are asked!* Please remember to do this. To receive and follow through is of critical importance, but do remember to <u>ask.</u> Your appreciation is warmly received and your follow through is applauded with zeal at many levels. However, the key is always to use your freewill to *choose.*

There is a children's song used to teach the letters of your alphabet. The alphabet is the foundation of the written words in your languages. What we desire you to learn to use is what is the foundation of manifested self-awareness. Just as you must learn to apply the alphabet to written language and combinations of sound to speak the language, you must use the principles that form the foundation for directing the flow of thought into the coagulated energy that creates what is experienced as life. It is the utilization of the potentiality underlying all that is known at every level. This is accomplished through a process mentioned before and is reflected at the very basis of your ability to remain in your earthly form, breathing. In simple format it is drawn in through expansion of the lung, rest, contraction of the lung, rest and repeat. The lung is the vehicle of containment and motion. It in turn is contained within the totality of a greater conscious awareness vehicle, the body.

This is a pattern matrix that is repeated in endless variety. The stumbling block is to learn to appreciate this variety each time it is encountered and to remember that it is but a unique manifestation of the basic pattern matrix. This difficulty is especially true if there is distortion in the particular expressions encountered through experience. The more confrontational the experience, the more distortion is occurring, not in just one, but in both individuals. Distortion unfortunately ripples outward and encompasses groups of interacting individuals. When the interactive distortion becomes large enough, then in order to correct the distortion, a large number of those involved must return to the relearning *and application of* the basic fundamentals of manifested experience. Simply stated they must relearn and apply the universal laws. Guess where your planetary inhabitants are?

Fortunately you have at your disposal communications with a high potentiality of reaching vast numbers, at least at the moment. Mounting pressures of multiple layers of oppression are creating tension within those that can be reached and there are yet many ways of reaching them. 100 years ago this would not have been possible, even though there were fewer to reach. These communication possibilities have been named "mass media" for good reason. There is no reason why these cannot be utilized for a reason contrary to what was originally intended. Perhaps there was even help in bringing them into such widespread use. Could be! Guidance in many areas is available on request. Where are your requisitions?

The length of these daily messages depends on how much information can be received and assimilated and in the conciseness of the message format. Clarity and conciseness are the goals, with enough repetition to assure the information is planted in fertile ground. If not, then another approach is used. For the greater part of human consciousness, the substitution of a new focus within their awareness is all that is necessary. For others of you, much more is involved. You have committed to physical action and the conception and dissemination of this new focus. After all, someone has to plant the seeds of thought that comprise the foundation of this new paradigm before they can begin to grow, mature and re-seed themselves. If you are reading this information, then you are chosen. Now the ball is in your court and you will choose to be chosen or not. It is your freewill decision.

Our blessings are given as you process the information and provide it to others for their consideration. In your vernacular hang in there, the roller coaster ride is just beginning. You have not even gotten to the exciting parts. Just know you are strapped in and the ride will end. However, I doubt you will wish it had lasted longer. Not this time.

No. 30

The focus of these messages has been toward the dissemination of information that concerns the expansion of your understanding with regard to plans and appropriate attitudes and actions within group areas. There has been little information with regard to your personal experiences and application in that area. This was not to indicate that this area is of little importance. New age information, better called new thought which could be categorized even more accurately as "remembered thought", emphasizes the need to be balanced and chants "be in the now". In actuality, that is correct! As previously pointed out, all of the cycles within the cosmos/galaxy move toward and away from the center point of stillness or perfect balance. In order for the galaxy to be in balance, the cycles are moving within a balance of those moving away and those returning to each balance point. You could picture it as gyroscopes spinning and moving around a central gyroscope that remains in perfect balance and puts forth an energy pattern that holds all the smaller gyroscopes within its sphere of influence. Each gyroscope outside the central focus contains within it myriad smaller gyroscopes. In order for this entire system to continue in existence there must be an equality of energetic motion. If one gyroscope gets far enough out of balance to approach a point beyond its ability to return, then counter balancing must take place within the whole system with the focus of holding it within the range of safety. This is, of course, an over simplified picture, but gives you some understanding. It allows you to picture Earth at its tilt of 23 degrees approaching a point of losing its ability to return to balance.

Consider that within the gyroscopic picture of Earth, there are 6 billion tiny gyroscopes each spinning on their own axis: the balance of these influences the balance of the larger one. If most of these are out of balance, then of course the larger one cannot remain in balance. Grasping this picture leads you to the understanding that the 4th universal law is that of balance. One pattern of thought that holds powerful influence in the balance or imbalance of personal expression is that of past, present and future. Since all are necessary for various reasons of survival and progress, they are embedded within the ego observer mode. You remember the burn and so do not touch the stove again. You desire to build a larger house for your family so you envision the steps your future must contain in order to attract that experience, and so you migrate between the two. However, there is the moment of now that you experience that is neither past or future. That is your balance point. It is your place of rest. You return there during each sleep cycle. There was a time as the planet revolved in the cycle of light and darkness, when all were active or resting in unison which brought greater balance to the whole. With the advent of artificial lighting, this balancing pattern is no longer present. Mankind now has constant activity first with the "industrial age". Now in the "technology age" even within the homes the hours of rest within a family are varied. A balancing technique is practiced in what you call the Far East and is called meditation. The new age group quickly adopted it. Techniques are often distorted and the conscious awareness is overwhelmed with media clutter and unable to find the still point of balance within the combination of conscious and subconscious. Entering that still point allows for connection with the Soul and balance to be reached for at least a short time.

Balance is reached through the understanding and practice of three basic laws of the universe: attraction, deliberate creation and allowance. If you review the previous messages, you will find within the information suggestions for resolving this problematic situation of the population of Earth. In order to live the new paradigm of experience those participating will be required to focus within present time. Only the framework will be known and it must be fleshed out through "living it into existence" experience by experience. This will require living within present moment reality. Within this focused group experience balance will be attained. The past cannot be applied and the future will be unknown. That will leave only the present.

Let us consider the galactic cycle completion. Is it only a momentary instant that is available to accomplish a grand ascension or a ghastly dimensional crash? That depends. Again we return to your fixation of experiencing measured blocks of sequential events. Experience within what you call the present moment is a misnomer, an inapplicable designation. When you are focused *into* what you are thinking or doing with no awareness of any other activity, you "lose track of time". Each of you has experienced that. Only by looking at your time tracking device called a clock do you have any idea of what the time might be, other than the presence or absence of sunlight. If each of you were totally intrigued with what you were doing, that was your only required focus and there were no seasons to concern you, would you care what day it was? If that intriguing subject opened the door to another and another, would you care what day or what time it was? I doubt it. If you were in balance, would sleep be necessary? What about food? What about recreational pursuits? Aren't all of these necessities really just a search for balance?

This is not suggesting that you become breatharians. These are simply ideas to intrigue your imaginations. Your experiences are so far out of intended balance that it is difficult for you to imagine what balance during wakeful experience is like in 3rd dimensional format. It is far more pleasant than you know. No wonder you desire to leave this dimension thinking that respite is only to be found elsewhere. Without balance of the 3rd dimensional experience you could not exist in higher dimensions in your body format and current self-awareness. *First* you must come into balance. Because you are all interconnected, individuals have insurmountable problems maintaining balance even if it is achieved. It is necessary to bring a large number into balance to accomplish what is necessary in the bigger picture.

The bible warns you not to place "pearls of wisdom" before those who have no viable connection to their source of life. It is time to strike that idea from the books. It is time to do another 180-degree turn and to do it in practical, applicable terminology. The pattern has always been to hide it within religious and esoteric terminology so that only a few were privy to the information, lest it be lost through individual interpretations that might destroy it. Without written words, for few were literate, allegorical stories were the only method of disseminating even the basic understandings. These contained references to activities and other commonly known and understood references that were within that local cultural environment. Even these basic understandings became distorted when the stories were retold in cultural situations that had no reference points to those original understandings.

We find ourselves of necessity reintroducing the basics. A good place to begin a new beginning, don't you agree? Attraction, intention and allowance leading to balance through application within experience. A doctorate in those positively leads to ascension to higher dimensions. Welcome to the ascending team!

No. 31

We are entering the period of time that leads to the beginning of the shift of energies that will begin the days of tribulation. Unfortunately some of the predictions that have been made reflecting the plans of the dark side will manifest. Though they seem to indicate that the situation is irreversible, it certainly is not. This will be a time in which it will be critical that those of you who are privy to the behind-the-scenes maneuvers of which you are part hold faithfully to the understanding and belief that they do indeed exist and are positively laying the foundation for the new paradigm. This new pattern of experience can be pictured as a shimmering castle coming forth amid a scene of frantic confused activity. It is at first very dimly seen. Though this is hardly the pattern of what the new paradigm will resemble, it instead draws on the Camelot myth as a recognizable fantasy containing within it desirable dreamlike ideals. It is a process of it rising through the mists of focused imagination in the midst of what appears to be reality. This is the understanding that we desire to trigger. If you are not a Camelot buff, then choose some other picture.

The Phoenix perhaps, but choose for it to be transformed and to rise before the ashes stage. We would emphasize the recognition that the desirable already is manifesting before the undesirable has disintegrated. The focus of even a few with belief and knowingness that it does indeed exist and is coming forth is of critical importance. By choosing different pictures but the same focus then the process is held in place until the purpose is defined and becomes the ideal.

Defining the purpose will not be an easy process. Many versions will be proposed before ideal wording can encompass it. This is meant to encourage ones to begin, for the first step must be taken so that progress can be made toward the goal of bringing it forth. It is the brevity and the universal appeal of it within the diversity of 6 billion beings that is the key. Though it seems impossible, we assure you it is possible. We remind you to ask for guidance and help at these sessions. Egos must be in their observer states for the credit of writing will go to no one individual. It is the desire that it comes forth in perfection that must be the motivation. It shall stand alone in its purpose of encompassing the foci present on earth into a focus of expression into greater experience. Again we remind you of the breathing process. It will be taken in by the conscious awareness, contemplated and expressed outward through desire for its manifestation into each personal reality and held dearly while it happens. We wish it were other than a lifeline for drowning beings, but that is the experience you have created.

It is through an approach encompassing universality of scope that the encompassing appeal shall be addressed. The focus on this aspect will begin to draw the feeling of oneness to the beings on the planet. A realization will begin to dawn that all are facing the same dilemmas. As the itchy feeling that something ominous is present continues to intensify, this feeling keys understandings that the causes of it are beyond local, regional or national scope. The oppression is being felt with greater and greater intensity.

What about the indigenous peoples? As we have mentioned before, they already know. Their "shamans" already have the message and are aware that a new paradigm is being born. They are steps ahead of you and are already at work on its expression. Their people are aware and already in harmony with the process. Do not be concerned for them. Survival is their way of life. You may find yourself wishing you had incarnated into a more indigenous way of life in the days ahead. (I did say may!) Inasmuch as all have incarnated from the same source, you are indeed connected and do communicate at subtle levels.

The mass consciousness (awareness) is malleable through coercion, but always certain levels of it remain connected to the source. It is through these connections that we can achieve subtle changes that will lay the groundwork for future shifts at the conscious levels. The oppressors must work with the levels of the mind while it might be said that we have available the levels of the "heart." The heart feels. A feeling can transform the beliefs held by the mind. When the feeling vibrates within the being at a certain level, it overrides the belief and the being simply tosses it out and follows the feeling to a new conclusion. The feeling of oppression is soon to override the insistence of the mind that all is well and that big brother government will work things out for the benefit of all. The magician is about to lose his veil of darkness and be seen in the full light of recognition, and it may not be at the time of his choosing.

Inasmuch as you live within time as your controlling focus, we must deal with it. The sequence of linking interfacing actions and events now enters a phase of critical importance. It is important that each of you feel the inspiration, the divine urge, to push ahead with this project. The dominos are in place and it will take but a nudge for them to begin their sequential trip. The placement of the final few must be preempted in order that the dark plan is unable to be carried to its planned conclusion. If a critical few can be removed, then the planned sequence will go awry and glorious confusion will result, the perfect time for the new paradigm to rise amid that confusion. Its conception must, however, have been completed and the birthing process well underway at the subtle levels.

It is difficult for the information contained in these messages to stress the importance of various facets without becoming repetitive. We also are aware that some are reading these that have not had access to the prior information, thus we attempt to make them at least somewhat inclusive. The window of time available to complete the second phase that is focused toward the completion of the worded purpose is continually shrinking. Therefore, we feel it necessary to continue to prod and poke lest it close without its completion. Chaos would then indeed reign and the birthing of the new paradigm could become unimaginably difficult. The period of chaos could stretch on for a painfully long time in your counting. *It is not this information that is important, it is the conception and completion of the writing of the purpose!* We do not want this information on file in your Library of Congress. We prefer it to be exchanged on a personal, need-to-know level. It is purposefully written so as to exclude words that trip the communication scanners so that it may yet spread easily to the chosen ones. We wish to be very clear about this. Our translator spends much time in the thesaurus mode looking for synonyms so word patterns are varied within each document. What appears to be but a few paragraphs involves much dedicated attention to this facet of caution. The purpose of this information weighs heavily on this conscious awareness, however commitment carries the process forward day by day. We are finding that commitment matched in like manner by the readers of it and are grateful indeed.

It is your resolve to bring this new archetype of experience into being that holds the progress made in place so that the building of the pattern can continue. Visualize the pattern of a snowflake only now beginning to crystallize from a drop of water. Just the very beginning of one corner of what will be a unique picture is happening. You are not only watching the creation of something uniquely beautiful, you are providing the focus that will cause it to happen. How could you avoid continuing to be an important part of this beautiful demonstration?

No. 32

When the time arrives for what could be termed the crash of all your systems of communications, utilities and supplies, there will be turmoil and confusion of massive proportions. It behooves you who are well aware of this possibility to survey your personal situations and to make contingency plans. It is amazing to us that this information is known but each assumes that it will happen around them but not to them. You are aware of the existence of various mechanisms that would provide at least minimum replacements for your utility needs; even coordinated systems are available. The project will not make the shift in consciousness before this breakdown of current lifestyle. There will be a period of chaos. How long that will last depends on the completion of phases two and three, the conception of the new paradigm and then the spread of it through the conscious awareness of your brethren. As you can deduce for yourselves, communications are relatively easy before the breakdown, and difficult at best after it. It is critical that you truly realize and begin preparing for this advancing menace with as much focus and dispatch as possible. We are long past the "I can hardly wait for it, but I don't have time to prepare for it just yet" syndrome. It is necessary for you to look carefully at your priorities and to remember that you have made commitments that involve the survival and transcendence of as many of your willing brethren as possible. This does mean that they have to be occupying their bodies for this to be successful. This is indeed a heavy responsibility, but we again remind you that all possible help is available if you but ask and "move your feet".

It would appear that it is necessary to also remind you that the discussions of phase 2 must be conducted in places that are not likely to contain listening wires. It is suggested that you view the movie called "Enemy of the State" and listen carefully when the character Brill describes the capabilities of the electronics. He goes through the list at top speed and so you must be listening carefully. It was also given on TV when the filming process of the movie was reviewed. Brill, in the movie, reminds the hero that the capabilities he is listing were available many years previously, however the capability to apply them in a massive manner was not possible until recently, but the added sophistications since exceed what is demonstrated in the movie. All of you are being observed and when you gather, you can be sure your discussions are of interest. We would prefer that this project continue unnoticed for as long as possible. If this sounds melodramatic, so be it. Ask for discernment and then view the movie and you will understand.

As our arrogant planners flaunt their methodology before your eyes assuming that sleeping minds have little discernment between programming and entertainment, there is no reason we cannot use this information to our advantage. When you ask for discernment within our purposes, the ability to interpret and to envision ways of applying the Laws given you will provide avenues avoiding their entrapment techniques. As all-encompassing as they appear, they are inventions of opposite focus and thus contain the elements of self-destruction. Just as Divine purpose contains within it the impulse for self-expansion the opposite contains the tendencies of self-destruction. When the negative polarity is expanded, then its innate tendencies are magnified, just as the opposite is true within the positive polarity. It is within the path between the two that the spiral of evolution exists.

It is important to note here that the meaning of the word "evolution" has been purposely distorted by implanting the idea that evolution and adaptation are synonymous. Animal life and even human life at one level adapts. Evolution refers to the spiral of spiritual experience through (think holographically) its return trip to the source. Here you can see a correlation of spiral to spirit and holographic to holy.

When the appropriate moments arrive, you will have the discernment to bring forward into your conscious awareness that prickly feeling that causes you to move to a more appropriate place and it will be available. Planning ahead does not work; it is necessary to be flexible and move in the moment. It is spontaneity that provides the atmosphere in which creation moves without restriction. Since creation is what you are about, then it is important to move within the framework of purpose as spontaneously as possible. Though it would seem that opposites are at counterpoints, indeed this is combining the polarities in a complimentary fashion allowing for the spiraling effect that is desired for movement in a balanced fashion. Polarities are not limited to extreme opposites as in black and white, on and off, good and bad, etc. Pink and gray are opposites, but of a different intensity. These intensities are available in abundance to apply, and through this principle diversity within a focus is accomplished.

How does this apply to the project at hand? It is through the diverse contributions toward the goal of completing phase two that the appropriate composite will come forth. Each session will be a think tank of spiraling ideas toward the goal fueled by combining the individual minds into an empowered group focus. It is the addition of the group focus that gives the increased power of the creative presence. Because the creator is not a personal presence at the 3rd dimensional level, he cannot be literally present, but the combination of focus provided by the shared common goal brings forth a greater power, particularly when numerical combinations are observed. The common language of creation is mathematical formulation. The practice of numerology touches upon how these formulations apply to individual lives. Spontaneity is allowing the conscious awareness to relax so that harmony with these foundations of existence will bring forth the desired results within the framework of defined purpose. The purpose of these think tank sessions provides the framework to bring forth a greater purpose that in turn will be the framework for the new paradigm. It will be the framework to provide for individuals to continue the process within their own experience. This may seem simple enough, however the strategy, it is in the understanding and follow through of the steps within the universal laws. Allowance is the most difficult to incorporate. Rising above the need to control is the leavening of the loaf so to speak. Volumes could be written regarding this, but it would not change anything. It is in the doing that it is accomplished. It is the doing of this one facet that opens the door to the transcendence of this dimension. The ability to apply this principle is built upon the use of the previous two and through the application of all three, the fourth is reached and bingo, you are there at the point of choice. To go or not to go! Graduation requires the release of attachments, then not now. Just as you have been misled regarding your ego, so have you been misled regarding your attachments? There is a difference between attachments and addictions. That is for you to discern and now is the time to release the addictions. You must ask yourself what it is that you think must remain in your experience and what it would be pleasant to have, but not absolutely necessary. You will be surprised if you take a few moments to make even a brief list of your technological wonders and contemplate what life will be like without them. You will then be prepared for your not so distant future. This is not to say that to plan to provide for the *basic* necessities is addiction rather than wisdom. Here again ask for discernment.

We remind you that it is our concern for all that motivates us to share as much guidance as possible, for this project is of critical importance. The creator is non-preferential in the desire to retain every fragment; we however value our ground team greatly. Friendship is a wondrous part of the shared experience of self-aware manifested fragments. You don't remember us, but we remember you!

No. 33

The days are now upon us for gathering the focus that will bring about the transformation of the mass consciousness. It will be an interesting process of inter-linking various consciously begun projects at different places on the planet. There are more than one ground crew with purposeful assignments. While it is natural to feel that what one person or one group is attempting is too little too late, this is not the case. All are now in place, or nearly enough so that the concerted beginning can be initiated. It is necessary that the resolve, intent and purpose be held securely within the scope of each of you, as the days ahead may seem discouraging. You must hold to your commitment with a calm and trust that does not waver. This experience is a manifested reality that must be dealt with inside that reality. The game must be continued on until completion. It can no longer be changed or delayed. Humanity is sinking into greater fear and confusion furthering the plans of the manipulators at a rapid pace. The spiritual levels of each are becoming more and more inaccessible and the reaction of the spirit expressing through the body to this process will continue to reflect through the reaction of the planet also. It is not a pretty picture from our perspective. It is not our intent to focus your attention into this picture but it is also necessary that you are aware of what you are working within. It is unfortunate that it has had to proceed this far into the levels of suffering before the consciousness becomes vulnerable and desperate enough to pause and reflect that enough is enough. Perhaps now enough can be reached with the desire to bring this situation to an end to be willing to accomplish it through a total change of engrained habitual reactions.

The locking mechanism has been what has been called "the opium of religion". The religious doctrine of "ours is the only way, and all else is wrong" has literally created cells within a dungeon of ignorance with every modern religious sect present and accounted for. This is not to say that some truth is not present within them, but there is not enough either within any one, or even a composite of the truth known within all of them, now to guide mankind in anything but unending circles of frustration. The innate desire is always within each to progress toward the goal of transcending this entrapment within the 3rd dimension and now religion offers no way to continue the journey. The aspiration of each soul extension as it incarnates on Earth is to assist in bringing this situation back into balance. Each desires to *become* part of the pivotal pebble in the pond, but instead is caught in the entrapment of the heavy oppressive pattern of energies and become part of the chorus calling out for assistance. The assistance can not come from without; it must come from within through self-empowerment, not for the purpose of placing the self over and above others, but in the genuine desire to inspire others to follow suit. In this way, these individuals come into harmony with the creative flow and with the focused conscious desire of those who are dedicated to this purpose that have accomplished this transcendence before. Unfortunately the situation has reached such a sad state that dedicated ones of higher dimensions have now volunteered to incarnate and act on behalf of the inhabitants and set into motion a wave of self-empowerment on the planet. These volunteers are numerous and await the triggers planted within their awareness to remember their roles. The time has come for this to begin!

Now is the time for these self-appointed ones to lead mankind from being into *becoming* what was intended. Human being is a misnomer; each is a human becoming! Knowing this and referring to themselves in this way, each would be constantly focused upon the true purpose of incarnation. Then the internal cry of those on the planet and the planet herself in this moment of time would become "I am a human (god-man) *becoming!* Help me to do this! Then response is possible. It changes the focus from "I am a victim, help me!" which implies help me to continue being a victim, to a focus of desire for self-empowerment. After centuries of calling for someone or some ritual or miracle to accomplish the impossible, man has been unable to figure out that it must come from within his own awareness and the empowering of himself so that it can be accomplished. Instead the self-empowerment urge was distorted into self-aggrandizement and the result is seen all around you. The shift of your own consciousness toward your desire for this end has brought forth your ability to attract these messages. As the wake up triggers are tripped, the ripples of the pebble shall become waves. Then the action shall begin and many levels of links shall form and wheels shall begin to turn. A beleaguered mass consciousness shall experience a shift as will the planet. This will not be *the shift,* but will be the beginning of the necessary upliftment that must precede that process.

Keep in mind the vibratory level of the mass consciousness. No inhabitant of planet Earth could survive a shift to 4th dimension at this time. No amount of meditating and listening to channeled entities has accomplished this feat. It must be a shift in self-perception and focus of the purpose of this incarnation in great numbers to accomplish this, as the flow now is downward in vibratory rate into disease and death. To halt this movement and change its direction will require a shift of major proportion. The normal vibratory rate of a human body has been determined to be between 62 and 68 MHz. The brain functions optimally between 72 and 90 MHz. When the body vibration lowers to 58 MHz it can "catch a cold"; at 57 MHz the flu; 55 MHz candida, 52 MHz Epstein Barr; 42 MHz cancer and at 25 MHz death begins. By considering the health problems of your friends and family, you can begin to get a true picture. Our interesting negative planners simply lower the MHz of someone they would like to eliminate through their recently devised methods. Within a short period of time, the body either develops a fatal disease or if lowered enough, death occurs and whatever disease already present is the excuse. Allopathic *medicine* (a misnomer), chemical prescriptions, lower the MHz of the body. Radiation from TV and computer screens lowers the MHz, and consuming processed and canned foods, which have 0 MHz to support the body, continue the process. Starvation is the least subtle of the ways to lower the MHz and bring on the lowering of the mass consciousness before each dies, in that way these make their contribution to this descending cycle. The human body has amazing adaptive abilities, but the onslaught of ways to bring down the vibratory level to tie you to this planet has reached a critical point. The good news is that the shift in focus of purpose by the critical mass within the encompassing planetary consciousness can go beyond removing a few critical dominos as placed by the interesting planners. It could reverse the way they fall thereby releasing the lowering process and allowing the MHz of the bodies to increase. Now that is an interesting supposition to consider!

The picture as it is at the moment is beyond discouraging; it is appalling. However, in playing out various scenarios in holographic possibilities it is not at all hopeless. The keys lie in the cards held by the "ground crew". How these are played will determine which of the scenarios are available to ensure success. Keep playing! The last game has just begun and the Creator never gambles. He only plays the sure bets. After all he made up the game and he never forgets the rules. You can rely on that! His turn to shuffle and deal is about to come up. Don't wait for it to happen elsewhere. Be here now!

No. 34

At the point in your timing when this project was initiated, there was a very small window in which to begin the process. Once the idea was grasped and acted upon, the next window encompassing moving into the process was much larger. This step allowed for the contact of various new individuals to be made aware and to continue the enlarging of the window. The addition of other minds grasping the basic idea and focusing their intention of participating has continued opening the window to allow for the continuing inclusion of additional participants. The expansiveness of this movement allows the process to come into harmony with the expression of divine order, which is expansive in its very nature. The momentum of the outward movement of this information forms the basis for continuing this harmonious flow and insures the divine participation that is essential to success. It is important that you realize the key to success is in expansive outward movement. It is the combination of grasping the various aspects of this intended change of attitude and focusing it through the needed number of points of individual awareness. The importance of these aspects is the establishment of an outward flow and maintaining this flow. New contacts must be made by as many of the recently contacted individuals as possible to keep this expansive flow in motion. As memories are keyed to think of other appropriate people not yet contacted, then ones can continue to make additional contacts. This insures that those without commitment to carry the "Letter to Garcia" do not impede this essential outward expansion.

If these messages were to be sent out to new contacts that are considered to be ones sure to follow through and actually continue the flow, it would perhaps be appropriate to send the first few as an introductory packet. A cover note suggesting that if theirs is a real commitment, then on request more of the messages will be provided. This would allow a spread of the cost for reproduction and mailing so that it would not be burdensome to a few. Each committed one would in all probability make only a few *appropriate* contacts. This also allows for anonymity and protection. It is assumed that only those known and deemed appropriate would be contacted so that discussions could be carried on in the groups of 3s, 7s and 12s (This is to again remind you of the numerical power available within divine mathematical order.) It is entirely appropriate that attempts to formulate a possible statement of purpose should be made at small group levels. The more of these attempts that are made, the sooner the "perfect one" will stand forth. When that happens, that group will be totally aware that completion has been accomplished for that phase. What to do next will also be drawn into that group awareness attracted by the power of the fusion of all the input from the totality of the groups. (Here again you are reminded that thought thinks within and upon itself when it is in divine harmony.) How many participants are necessary for this parenting phase? That depends on three factors: who, how quickly the phase is initiated and the productive discussions actually taking place. The ball is in your court. Responses in terms beyond intellectualizing the shift in perception are the keys. We can participate further when you return the ball to our court. In the meantime, we are limited, in this project, to this flow of information and encouragement.

The overall view from our perspective is somewhat encouraging. The plans of the interesting participants of opposite purpose continue right on schedule. It is important that the view of our focus is one of action and <u>not</u> reaction. It is in the ability of our group to have a balanced dual perspective that spreads with the awareness of our project. This will sustain the momentum. There must be an awareness of the awesome inevitability of the probable success of their "plan" and a balancing awareness that ours is the only shift available that offers the power to bring release from the intended horrendous future. If followed with dedication and resolve through application of the universal laws of attraction, focused intention to create a new paradigm of experience and allowance through lack of resistance, return to balance and harmony <u>must</u> be the end result. Only through this format can the help so ardently sought by suffering humanity be provided. All of the above discussion of bringing others into the awareness of the possibility of creating a new paradigm of experience for this planetary focus, when simply stated, is that the *return to personal responsibility* is the only avenue leading to success. As individuals assume responsibility, group responsibility through cooperation is the inevitable result. Those unable to move beyond the desire for personal material gain and the need to control the proceedings and the outcome will soon drop by the way side. If discernment is used in choosing appropriate contacts, those may be considered but not contacted.

If at first appropriate names do not come into your awareness, as you continue to desire to participate, names and coincidental contacts will "happen". The law of attraction works! Just hold the desire in your consciousness, especially at times of least attention to other activities. As you retire, when you awaken, at the end of meditation or intentional prayer times are appropriate. The more often it comes into your mind and you *feel* strongly about desiring to be part of this positive exercise in participation with the creator within his modus operandi, the greater the contribution you will make. Commitment and resolve are the buoyant qualities that hold this desire on the surface of your consciousness so that opportunities for you to participate are attracted to you. Through this process you will indeed be a blessing and a focused beam of light in this darkened world. A spotlight spreads into a larger and larger circle at the end of the beam. A greater understanding through your choice to become a part of this project will allow you to spread this light of understanding in the midst of a darkening world. Your inner confidence and the peace of knowing that something powerfully new is already being created as the present reality is changing is a powerful positive pole. This attitude will attract to you those desiring change and ready to transcend the victim state. You will be the pebble within your own pond of experience. Your service will continue to expand to other levels of experience. Don't plan on a dull and boring life from this point on.

Your participation in this project will bring with it personal rewards. Recognized sainthood is not one of them. Changes in consciousness will happen as you participate and as your body is able to accommodate them. Those of you who continue to dishonor the living temple of your spirit will miss out on some of these rewards. Caffeine, carbonation, a diet of prepared (over cooked) foods, etc. require you to reconsider your priorities. Many of you are without a mate that results in choosing to eat out. Consider your choices and opt for food cooked for shorter periods and include raw foods. If you eat at home, many supermarkets now carry some organic foods. Overeating causes the body to use its energy digesting rather than using it for more productive modes. Smaller amounts of nourishing foods allow the body to use its available energy in other activities and to possibly require shorter sleep periods.

Much is being asked of you, but knowing you incarnated herein this lifetime to participate in this project allows you to stop wondering "why me, why here and why now?" This in itself will bring you to change your priorities. As participation in it becomes your priority, those activities that are not important to it will shift out of your life. It is the way it works. Will this take over your life? We would hope not. It is where the action is and so your life will take *it* over. A different and energizing perspective! The taking on of personal responsibility and moving within the flow of creation for the purpose of expanding creation, bring rewards of a personal nature as well to the larger picture. It is a most enjoyable experience. As you participate you will remember how it feels to be in balance and harmony and this will assist you in knowing and making your necessary contributions to the wholeness of the project. To bless is to be blessed indeed!

No. 35

It is interesting from our perspective to see that you are busily building a reservoir of energy that is standing in stagnation. There is a growing number of people aware of the paradigm project, but few if any have sat down to play at composing what might be their personal idea of a statement of purpose. It is as though you must wait until you meet in some type of formal meeting to accomplish anything. Where is personal responsibility in this response? It would seem to me that bringing your personally defined idea along with you would bring a different level of intent to a meeting to define a purpose. It was hoped that this would be a natural outcome of the suggestion that you begin this process for your own salvation. Do not assume that your ground crew status will be enough. You are in 3rd dimensional experience and are governed by it the same as all other inhabitants of the Planet Earth. If personal responsibility is the keynote, then operate within it, especially with regard to the project if you hope to achieve its purpose.

We are finding it difficult from the perspective of our experience to comprehend just how difficult it is for you to experience within the vibrational level of Earth. The combination of planned lowering techniques being applied to all aspects of earthly existence is inevitably lowering the vibration in measurable calibrations. It is the concerted effects of the multiple techniques that are accomplishing this. The critical mass of humans now within the control of these combined techniques will soon be reached. It is important for you to have the understanding that the critical mass point needed for evil intent is different than it is for intent of upliftment. This cannot be calculated in simple percentages, for the degree of evolvement of each soul and its extensions must be considered in this calculation. As the vibratory rate descends the critical mass point ascends while the opposite is true from our point of view. Lowering the vibratory rate is much more difficult than raising it. A simple realization can cause a jump in vibratory rate. So why don't we just trigger a big planetary realization and fix the whole thing? As the vibratory rate lowers the brain synapses become more and more impaired. Also the use of sugar substitutes such as "Equal" is slowly destroying the ability of the brain to function as they destroy the nerve endings. These can and do cross the blood brain barrier. Further, low fat/high sugar bearing carbohydrate diets are starving the brain cells. All of this is part of the plan: remember they understand the functions of the physical body well enough to be able to develop techniques to weaken the connection of the being to its vibratory source in hopes it can be broken at their moment of choosing. May we stress that you think carefully about this information and that you read your labels and take *personal responsibility* in the care of the bodily functions necessary to participate in this project. Beyond that which was mentioned in this message and the previous one, the remaining critical factor is the pH level of your body and your blood.

If you are serious about wanting to return to higher dimensional experience then you are required to master the 3rd dimension and the completion of this project is recommended as your ticket. Personal responsibility is being responsible for your personal expression of this life experience, starting with your body temple. To do that now you will need to think independently of what is being touted in your media and by the medical community. Even most alternative "professionals" are versed in less than holistic understanding and offer only partial assistance with their expensive products. Massage is a pleasant interlude but is not a replacement for the personal responsibility of regular gentle exercise.

Are we lecturing you? What is offered is by way of guidance. If you take it in any other way, then you are reacting through the distorted ego function. It depends on whether you can act rather than intellectualize. The ego has been distorted so that it loves to pontificate and to excuse so that personal responsibility can be avoided. It is so much easier to talk that to do when changing established patterns is involved. It can be overcome by ignoring it and placing the focus beyond the chaos of change and instead on visualizing the end result. Pictures bypass the intellectualizing process and are the true language of the brain. In order to come up with a statement of purpose, the parenting groups must spend personal time visualizing (dreaming) what each can conceive through imagination (going within the mind of God) and then attempting to put it into concise wording. The process can begin with words, then mental movies, then words again, etc. This would bring into practice purposeful meditation, a wonderful tool of higher dimensions. I believe it has been referred to as *"becoming* that which you desire". Those known as shamans and oracles use this technique and walk in two "worlds". There are nuances of the universal laws that support the intended purpose of experiencing your way back to the source of all. It is an adventure offering challenge and joy far beyond 3rd dimensional physical challenges. These leave the empty feelings that ones feel can only be filled with more challenging experiences that bring the same frustrating results of emptiness. The paths of learning are blocked and mankind on Earth is left chasing its nonexistent tail and being led in a downward spiral.

Continuing in our focus of accepting personal responsibility, it is important to consider another aspect. The ideal of personal responsibility is perceived as being heavy on the responsibility aspect. It would serve humanity better if the accent were on the personal aspect. Again personal has been distorted to assume the meaning of selfishness which is translated from the deliberate focus of denying that one can create independence and must take what is needed from someone else. The bankers on your planet illustrate this law of the proposed negative system and carry out this concept to the extreme. This group is not only visualizing their planned result, but is living it now. This increases the available energy required for their plan to move forward. Your bible has a statement within it that reads something like "The rain falls on the just and the unjust. How do you feel about that?" The rain refers to the universal laws working within the focus of either polarity. You are programmed to think that the negative pole is always "bad". Within the context of the whole this is not true. There is no electricity (energy moving) without both poles. It is distorted use beyond the norms of balance that are at issue in this instance. Personal has the true meaning of the harmonious expression of the fragment of creator energy expressing radiantly by continuing the flow of expansive energy into whatever dimension it is within. The word was devised within the focus of referral to the fragments as the family of god, perSONal. Again the masculine reference because it is within the perception of expansiveness being a masculine aspect. In other words, personal responsibility exemplifies the willingness to be a flow of expansive energy within the realm of your pattern of experience. With the cycle of energy surrounding you moving in an opposite directional flow, you must swim upstream so to speak to accomplish what you intend.

Hopefully these messages will provide a convenient rock on which you can stand above this flow in order to get your equilibrium, gain strength through resolve and then start to gather the rocks necessary to build a dam to divert the flow in a new direction. Yours is a holy project reflecting the wholistic nature of how "it all" works. Within your sequential focus it must come together piece by piece, but it may not, in true reality, work that way. This is why it is so important that you trust the process especially when you think things are not working as they should be. Just do your part and all will come into place! Trust!

No. 36

Let us continue with these messages for a few more sessions. These pertain to the parenting phase of project new paradigm. The ball then is in your court for action. Either you pick up the ball and move into actually doing the conception of the "babe" or not. Certainly we have been making every effort to encourage your participation. If it is necessary for the pebble to be dropped at the next level, you are going to have an interesting ride on space ship earth. This is a further wake up call. The snooze bar is reaching the end of its program. If you are reading this information, you are a part of the ground crew and need only realize it is time to drop your disguise and begin your mission. The flight crew cannot land until the field is ready and the invitation is issued. As suggested before, begin formulating and dreaming scenarios within your own personal awareness. This triggers the resonance of the law of attraction. "In the beginning there was the thought and the thought became flesh."

It is a matter of bringing the information shared previously into a cohesive understanding that allows you to operate within the appropriate process. Since the paradigm can only be brought forth within a holographic format that resonates in harmony with the wholeness of creation, it would seem logical that you must understand the basic parameters required to ensure success. Since this involves feeding this information to you in bits that can be pondered and assimilated, it ends up spread over many pages. You are then left to combine the bits into a composite that formulates a sensible basis for moving into the creative process with confidence.

It will be necessary for you to assume the study mode and reread these lessons in order to bring forth your own understanding and to formulate your personal foundation. There are nuances of the laws that will blossom into your awareness through the study-assimilation process. It would be convenient for you if we would simply provide you with an outline, but that would not allow the flowering process to be reached as an end result. It is nice to receive a bouquet and simply enjoy the beauty and the fragrance, but the growth process would be skipped. It is necessary that you "grow" your understanding. The Handbook of the New Paradigm is a precious treasure given to you so that you may step into your radiant stance of service and fulfill your chosen destiny in the history of Planet Earth. Through this suggested process the burden of responsibility will transcend into the pure joy of bringing "en-*light*-enment" to a world of darkness.

Within the holographic process is the element of maintaining the focus to enable manifestation to complete its intended cycle. The focus of thought is maintained for long periods of time (again staying within your reckoning mode) by setting the vibratory oscillations within a range that emanates sound. This is duplicated in crude form by your music. In purity it can be grasped as being of a crystalline bell-like quality. Tibetan bells give you an inkling of the reverberations that continue for long periods of time, beyond what the human ear can hear. Within a holographic context, a continuous vibration is set forth in an over unity mode carrying forth the expansive paradigm. Each holographic creation is unique, reminiscent of your snowflakes. There is present within each galaxy a continuous melody of bell-like sounds which is perceived in part by some and referred to as "the music of the spheres" which is a perfect description.

Earth is at the moment quite out of tune. Contemplate the resonance of the crystalline music of the spheres and then think of punk rock. That might be thought of as the resonant sound of the planned new galaxy. Would you want to live there all the time? Perfect resonance is attained through balance. This is the reason that rock music is so destructive to the balance of the young people. It is designed to be unbalanced and discordant in its basic construction. It reflects outward the inner imbalance of its composers and it enhances chaotic tendencies within the psyche of those spending long and frequent time listening to it. The bridge for this phase from romantic sexually stimulating music was the Beatles. Their early music contained melodies with a lesser amount of distortion as is demonstrated by the orchestral versions. It did however open the door for the more destructive distortions that inevitably followed. Again all part of the plan to slow and hold down the human vibration.

In order for you to conceptualize a higher dimensional experience, it is necessary that you have some understanding of the experience of it from the creational perspective. Holographic interaction is basic to this understanding. Current methodology to produce this phenomenon involves a beam of light focused through a transparency that produces a floating dimensional replica. In an existing holograph (you) conceive a thought of a desire to be reproduced in like holographic mode. This thought thinking (you) focuses by enlarging this thought with details that further define the holographic desire, and increases the energy of the beam-like thought with emotions of what the experience of enjoying this new holograph will be like therefore empowering it to come into form.

You call the holographic concept 3D or third dimensional. How then is the 4th dimension different? 3D encompasses the conception of height, width and depth, but involves no motion within the holograph of its own volition. (3D movies involve dimensional glasses. Virtual reality is also a manipulation.) The next step into 4th dimensional experience superimposes the living or vibratory dimension of action within the purview of the holograph itself. A true holograph is projected through thought, not by a mechanism. Since thought has the power to act upon itself with further thought, it is self-aware. A higher degree of self-awareness implies a higher vibratory rate or dimension of experience. The seeds of one dimension are planted within the lesser one.

This brings you to the understanding that you are already aware of being self-aware. However, this seed must be nurtured and cultivated in order to flower into transcending to a point of outgrowing its present placement through increasing its vibratory rate until it lifts itself into a dimensional shift allowing for greater opportunity to grow even more self-aware. What you are attempting to do is to cause this process to manifest on a planetary scale because earth's vibratory environment is so distorted that individuals can no longer accomplish it. Just as Moses had to cross the Red Sea at the exact moment of a planetary shift, this is timed at the exact moment of a galactic shift. How will you know? That is our job.

As usual, you are being reminded that unless you create a plug and pull it, some other backup plan will be employed that will bypass the opportunity for humanity to clean-up their own act and use it as a stepping stone for advancement. We continue to stress the power that you hold in the palm of your hands. It is such a gift to be in the position of assisting this planet and its inhabitants into a shift of such major proportion and it carries with it an opportunity for literally jumping up the vibratory scale. We can only bring the opportunity to your attention and act in an advisory capacity. You must be the ones to do it. It is not the first time you have participated in similar roles. This is the mission you have literally trained yourself to take part in, so don't drop the ball now. There is *nothing* more important in your current realm of experience.

No. 37

Progress is being made within the hearts and minds of those who are reading these messages. By progress we mean there is a shift within the consciousness that is reflected within the holographic activity that is you. In other words, the thought that each of you are, is thinking and acting within itself. Your psychologist/psychiatrists would say there is a shift in the data stored within your subconscious. The prayer given previously, *"I am a human becoming, help me to become!"* is powerful enough that simply reading it and considering it with a positive attitude begins the shift. The victim attitude is deeply ingrained within humanity as a whole. It shuts down the light of each child as soon as it is absorbed from the parental attitude. With the realization that victimhood is a falsehood and an idea to be released, the holographic pattern immediately begins to brighten. Use it as a mantra, especially when encountering situations that have in the past triggered what has been referred to as "giving away your power". These can be encounters with other people or life situations resulting from inappropriate decisions. The prayer wording allows a shift in attitude that reflects the intention of taking back that power. As it is practiced on a small scale within each individual life, then it becomes a tiny grain of sand in the mass consciousness that grows as others receive and begin to use this simple thought in their daily lives.

It might be appropriate to define mantra. It is a short series of sounds or words that brings about balance within what you call the subconscious awareness. Often the sounds are from ancient languages that are not consciously understood, but resonate at the DNA/RNA level of the body bringing about change in an outward flowing manner. The mantra as currently used is often an intuitive decision on the part of one person assigning it to another. Frequently the appropriate combination is not given and years of repetition bring little if any change. Some choose on their own with the same result. The use of the simple prayer, "I am a human becoming, help me to become", guarantees results. The most benefit is gained, not by setting aside a period and using continuous repetition, but by single statements made in connection with conscious recognition of thoughts, encounters or situations that are bringing forth your victim response. Remembering and thinking it several times during the day is also very helpful.

You each have victim responses and there are no exceptions. You simply deny you do in order to deny that you give away your power to an Ego that does not exist. Denial is the shield of the empowered Ego that fosters victimhood as a result. This prayer will end the deification of the ego. Ego is a function not a false god personality. "Thou shalt have no other gods before me." The number one false god is the falsely enthroned ego that you have been programmed to struggle against. A number of commonly used quotes are appropriate "That which you resist, persists." "That which you fear shall come upon you." etc. You have been programmed to turn everywhere but inward in self-contemplation that results in self-empowerment that in turn flows outward into expansive expression. Self-contemplation is not sitting and staring at your navel wondering "who, what and where am I?" It is practicing the use of the universal laws and contemplating the results of these applications in experience for the purpose of self-enlightenment. Each experience is a pebble in the pond of your life.

Your not so friendly perpetrators have added other layers of programming very effectively. You must not look inward or empower the self because that is "selfish". You are then "guilty" if you consider empowering the self because it is then implied that you will use the power to "overcome" others. This results in a distortion through misinterpretation early in childhood as each attempts to establish their innate tendencies to follow what gives them joy into greater expression. The distortion spreads into countless intermingling and inter-acting complicated behavior patterns that pass from one generation to another. The simple use of the prayer/mantra frequently within group/family situations by the participating members would bring dramatic changes. The wide use of it "wisely" would have phenomenal results.

The point of this segment of information is not as a sermon, but instead to illustrate how a statement of simplicity and appeal can bring forth change in a way that resolves and literally dissolves intermingled and interrelated distorted patterns of experience. If you doubt this, use the small prayer and observe what happens. The more you use it appropriately (wisely) the greater demonstration you will observe. Following the first few remembered uses of it, you will find yourself using it silently in situations as simple as being irritated because the waitress is slow. It changes your experience, which in turn changes hers. There will be big irritations that will slip by and later when remembered these are the most appropriate times to say it with meaning (emotion). It works!

It would seem that this series of messages could perhaps have been condensed down into a few simple statements that would be as effective as the small prayer. Perhaps, but would you have heard them? In observing human tendencies, especially ones with media overwhelm and information clutter, it is a matter of chipping away at the established patterns of the "read and toss" syndrome. Most who have awakened to the reality of the situation surrounding you are avid readers and listeners with this syndrome deeply patterned. The media overwhelm consists of constant repetition plainly presented and supported by subliminal key words and phrases. This places a shield of resistance at the subconscious level that then accepts the subliminal messages like arrows penetrating a target.

These messages have had to slowly penetrate this shield using repetition and realizations of truth as our arrows to penetrate the shield and to cause places in the shield to open so that the messages could be absorbed in the rereading of the same version but understood in a new light. Greater clarity and conciseness of particular true statements should augment this opening process. This doesn't indicate that your shield attempting to protect you from the media barrage is weakened, instead it is strengthened. The greater realization of the bigger picture of both aspects of your surrounding situation allows for conscious sifting of all the information you are inputting. The realizations of truth and your sincere commitment to the project have rearranged the content of the subconscious in a way similar to programs used so computer files can be rearranged allowing the disk space to be used in its most efficient configuration. This will be reflected in your life experiences. There may be some confusion, especially during your sleep patterns as this reconfiguration of your subconscious actually happens. For the more self-aware, it will be more pronounced and for a time, even troublesome. This process will allow you to absorb the important contents of the messages into a format at both levels of consciousness. It is like entering two interacting programs on a computer. Something like Word overlaying Windows, both contributing to a greater practical application available to the "user". How well it works depends on how well the user learns and applies its available unique applications. This is an apt analogy for careful consideration by serious users intending to take advantage of the opportunity to short cut older methods of "grubbing it out".

No. 38

There are many levels involved in the process of bringing forth the accelerated change in the consciousness of earth inhabitants/planetary awareness. The focus of the mass consciousness at the individual level is outward in contemplation of each one's environment. The deliberate teaching that the creator is a personality somewhere beyond the sky in the "heavens" making arbitrary judgements about which of the victim prayers deserves answering, is a picture of the structure inherent within the abhorrent plans being carried out all around you. It is constrictive in its focus, the opposite of expansive creation that maintains itself through an over-unity mode, meaning the flow brings forth an exponential increase of energy beyond what is focused into manifestation. This results through the inverse movement of the self-contemplative focus, which is within the intentional manifestation or the action of the 2nd universal law. It can again be likened to there being two sides to a coin. Through the intention of creating/manifesting there is the result of the manifestation and then the contemplation or experiencing of this process which is the self, contemplating as it experiences. This involves the 5 senses, ego observation and the contemplative thought process. Ideally all this moves through the individual life experience in a flow.

This is not to say that each individual would always create positive experiences. However, if the process was understood at the subconscious level, then the effects of an inappropriately caused experience would be contemplated. Through the necessary adjustments of attitude and intention, a lesson would be "learned" and the overall experience pattern continued with little trauma, greater wisdom gained and further upliftment of the energy vibration.

Through consideration of the ideal, it is easy to conclude that the planned reversal of this flow to create an opposite inclusive flow would end in something like your scientists' theory of the black hole, absorbing all available energies into a compacted mass. Why then have these planners not figured out the greater picture of the inevitable end of their endeavor? The enthroned ego with an addiction to power and control is seldom able to perceive logically. You perceive this type of distortion as insanity because of an individual's inability to follow the logical norm of the societal group. Sometimes it is because the creative thought process is far beyond this societal norm and sometimes it is ruled by distorted ability to perceive. This is both genetic and learned behavior through controlled indoctrination interchanged between the present generation and those following. The particular group holding our interest promotes longevity and positively believes in reincarnation. Each of the hierarchy is programmed at birth through magical methods to believe that they are a reincarnation through a long line of predecessors all committed to this project. Each generation is then perceived as being more empowered than the last. In this way, their project has continued on for what you experience as eons of time toward this important pivotal point.

This project, which deviates so far from the acceptable norm, has come into form through the use of the first two laws of the universe, attraction and focused intention. However, it is not possible for them to move out of the flow of expansive energy in a relaxed mode. The law of allowance is ignored. The only way for balance to be maintained is through rigid control of all aspects by planning and executing every detail to dovetail within their overall plan. Deviations are detected as quickly as possible and all haste is taken to remedy the situation by any means possible in the belief that the end justifies the means. This overview of the pattern of their plan does not indicate that it is any less formidable. Earth and its inhabitants are firmly within the grip of its influence and the situation must be *intentionally* resolved. It is beyond the point that containment would be appropriate while the inhabitants figured their role out. The control being exerted outweighs the possibility of this taking place without focused assistance. The focused assistance is manifesting, into the heart of their game, in the form of Project New Paradigm with its multi-faceted application of all four laws. You must contemplate the inside-out process concurrent with the outside-in process through the nuances of previously explained facets of creative flow to arrive at a picture of the game board. You will then be able to choose intelligently to join the play or not.

The play will be interesting to follow. One focus of play will be intense and controlled giving forth an aura of determined restraint, planning and examining every move. The other, relaxed allowing each play to be drawn through the wisdom of thought thinking resulting in calm game moves each flowing into the next in an expansive mode. The adversary considers that each play represents a shift necessary before another play can be conceptualized and focused into manifestation within the application supplied by the use of two universal laws as a self-governing factor. The balance as perceived by them is established control. Since their focus is restricted to using only two laws, using the third in an opposite mode makes the fourth impossible to attain. In other words, within our analogy, they are playing with only half a deck. There are slang references to insanity as playing with only half a deck. Quite appropriate!

There have been frequent uses of analogies within these messages. Each illustrates the understanding of two areas, the reintroduction of the universal laws and an overview of the game strategies in simple terms. We have attempted to add dimension to those understandings within succeeding messages. As you assemble these bits of information into blocks of understanding, you enhance your ability to contribute to the project. Commitment and resolve garner confidence in your day to day experience as you attract opportunities to participate. This releases the need to react toward the programmed individuals caught up in the negative focus and brings allowance into your experience. You know how the game is being played and can now perceive that you have the choice to participate intelligently resulting in a new sense of balance through purpose. Through returning to a familiar expansive expression, your sense of well being becomes magnetic and radiant. You are beginning the transcendent process.

The creative process takes advantage of every opportunity to continue its expansive mode. Your heart welcomes this wondrous opportunity and adds the dimension of emotion to the thinking level bringing forth outward dimensional expansion. This is how it works!

No. 39

There was a time that mankind experiencing on this planet brought all into balance. It was an experience that set what you might term the ideal into the consciousness at the planetary level. This then established the ability to recognize imbalance and allow for the desire to return to that ideal. This realization of what is and is not balanced experience comes from deep within the awareness. This singularity of focus is the controlling factor allowing the planet to remain within the orbital pattern of the solar system. What is perceived as gravity as it relates to the magnetism of the planet does not apply to the planets as they orbit within the solar system. This is a higher application of the law of attraction, or like being attracted to like. When there are similar criteria involved in the creative focus that brings a system into manifestation, that similarity is the basis for remaining within the field of focus. Inasmuch as there is a natural over-unity flow of energy accumulated, the system continues to expand and additional planets are formed. The process involved is not the point, only that you grasp the understanding that your scientists cannot understand what is at the basis of manifested creation without understanding the basic laws of the universe and the principle of thought thinking and acting upon itself independent of control. Once this basis is accepted, then the door to understanding is opened. It was never meant for man to gaze in wonder at what surrounds him, but that he should understand. The human brain is but a radio receiver that is capable of tuning into the flow of knowledge ever present in the creative flow. The magnetic field surrounding each of you is like an antenna, but your acquired belief systems cause you to unplug from the universal station and instead plug only into the (5) sensual environment. The spiritual aspect of the hu(man), the god aspect of self-awareness, is unknown to you through the stressed importance of material manifestation and the distorted influence of your religions. The adventure you search in vain to find is found in exploring the journey of the spirit that you are into manifested experience and in finding its every expansive return trip. This explains why each goal attained is never enough, and more and more must be attempted or lapse into discouragement and plan instead for a trip to the city of golden streets to take up playing the harp on a local cloud.

Humanity as it knows itself on Planet Earth at this moment is experiencing a degree of utter frustration that is incredible indeed. This can be compared to a balloon filling at an exponential rate toward the explosive point. The master planners of control are watching for this bursting point and planning its expansion with what they believe to be great care. However, just as balloons from the same package burst at different air pressure levels, neither can they be sure what the exact bursting point may be. It is a matter of how this released energy is directed that is the important point. Will it be as they choose or can it be self-directed by the mass consciousness of the awareness inside that bubble? Could the energy within the bubble be redirected from frustration to creation and deflate the balloon? They have no contingency plan to deal with these possibilities. It only requires one small hole in the dike to destroy the dam. Several or even many small holes insure and speed the process. Why not one big explosion? Allowing weak points to expand is within the expansive flow of creation, while deliberate destruction is not. Considering possibilities within your own life experience is self-contemplation, again within the expansive flow of experience. Does the focus of applying the law of attraction and deliberate manifestation of the opportunity for the weaknesses in their plans to expand include the destruction of the ones who would enslave or end your earthly experience by their choice? It is suggested to consciously withdraw participation by focusing instead on an entirely different creation project that will simply transcend the planned disaster. This would leave the perpetrators holding the bag and experiencing the other side of the coin, as fits into the experience of the law of attraction through their own use of it. This would be a wonderful demonstration of the universal laws in concept and application.

Conceptualization of the simple changes in how a situation is perceived and, using a change of the focus of intention, applying the universal laws that have brought forth the wholeness of manifested reality, is a big stretch of your understanding of how "things really are." When you reread this material, ask for the spiritual aspect, the source of your manifestation into this life experience, to give you discernment. Ask to **know** if this material contains truth and what are the applications of these truths that will serve you, your fellow inhabitants and the planet. It is your right to know if this is guidance or trash. "Ask and it shall be given unto you." This statement was not given to bring you material things directly but that you might receive knowledge (information) to be experienced into wisdom. It is appropriate to continue to paraphrase, "unto those, much will be given and from them much will be expected." When understanding is given, you are expected to apply the laws and to live within them in ever expanding application and further understanding. "Ignorance is no excuse before the law." The laws work whether you understand them or not. Intelligent intentional application is the best bet for an adventure that will keep you delightfully occupied, depending on your ability to overview your own experiences and see them in context. Attitude does determine your altitude.

There are many puzzle pieces within these lessons that will be assembled by each serious endeavor to do so. Amazingly these completed puzzles will each be a unique piece that will fit into the puzzle at the next level. You exist within a dimensional whole. Even the pieces are dimensional rather than flat. A necessary shift in how you conceptualize is available as a stepping stone for greater understanding. When you add dimension and life, which is thought thinking, to the game board, it lights up. Through your imagination you can begin to perceive movement within flow. Nothing is lifeless or stagnant. Every quark, atom and molecule is pulsing with thought and movement. Nothing is truly flat or solid. You cannot walk through walls in your manifested body at the density of 68 MHz or less. This should not be a mystery. When your brain vibration is 90 MHz or less, you are unable to tune your radio-like brain to the universal flow and receive the keys to the mysteries of galactic intentional focus. The possibilities of adventures leading to these experiences are encompassed within these lessons. Not all is directly presented for much is there to be contemplated and greater understandings brought forth through personal unique processes. Within the creator's flow all uniqueness is divergent and cohesive. Two sides of the coin, or should that be a visualization of something that is dimensional rather than flat, incorporating the polarities through expression and experience for the purpose of returning to balance and adventuring forth again. The practice of discernment is an inclusive nuance of self-contemplation of experience for the purpose of gaining wisdom and moving on into further expansion. A wise practice to apply frequently.

No. 40

When the ending of the millennium does occur, it does not do this on the date of your calendar. The cycles are not required to follow your calendar of the seasons. The basis of the cycles is not from the Earth perspective but from what you call the zodiac as Earth passes from one influence of the 12 aspects of experience to the next. The starting place of each planet's trip through these influences does not follow the conclusions drawn by astrologers but is determined by the mathematical equation of the solar system as it synchronizes with the master equation of the galaxy. It may then be assumed that the true ending of the millennium cycle is unknown other than in a general sense, and it is close to your calculated time, give or take a few months. The cycles shift at higher levels as the "heavenly bodies" (observable in the night sky, which is nearly impossible because of artificial lighting), **all moving in cycles** reach points for repetition to begin. This indicates ending and beginning within the conceptualization of finite thinking that is confined to the lower realms of dimensional experience. Each cycle may be thought of as a portion of a breathing process allowing for a rest period or a time spent at the zero point of balance before the shift. The zero (rest) point is the point at which each manifested creation partakes of an energy "feeding" process, or a gathering of new energy before it moves into the new cycle.

It is this available energy that the devious ones plan to utilize combining it with the separated soul energy they plan to gather. They perceive this will supply an additional over unity boost to bring about their planned shift from positive to negative. They also perceive that the control they are exerting will be accepted as the balance necessary for the energy transfer to occur at the resting point of the cycle shift. Magicians assume that their tricks are accepted as real by observers caught up in the process. Unfortunately for them, they are the ones caught up in their own deception. The creator and the creation do not observe the darkness of deception for all thoughts and plans are known.

Glaring reasons that humanity as it now experiences cannot in this moment exist in the higher dimensions are that thoughts and emotions are available to be read by all. Deception is impossible because intentions are fully known. This brings personal responsibility as the basis for higher dimensional experience into the light of logical understanding. Individuals sharing the same dimensional experience screen out inharmonious thought to allow balanced group experience. Focused thoughts are known and then what you call mental telepathy eliminates the need to slow the vibratory rate to vocalize thoughts. Since all at this level are consciously aware that their shared intention is participating in their return trip to the source of their own creation, the transition is not fraught with difficulty. Are their deviations? Of course, but normally these are worked through in a supportive environment. It is rare that an individual must be returned to a lower dimension.

As you begin to understand a larger picture of this point in the history of your planet and the segment of humanity that now resides on it, you can pinpoint your own experience within the scenario. If indeed you are a volunteer who has placed itself in a lower dimensional experience in order to assist the individuals trapped there, then it hardly seems fair that you must be bound by the confines of that dimension. Unfortunately that is how it works. However, it was understood when you volunteered to do this, there would be a point that you would be fully reminded who and what you are and of the agreement you made. In other words you were promised a wake up call. This is your wake up call.

No. 41

Now that this information has begun to be absorbed into your consciousness and the subconscious levels of your awareness are rearranging to allow an attitude adjustment a new focus is developing. The world you observe is changing before your eyes. There are three levels of awareness developing, the facade as presented to you, the activities of the magicians and the refocusing of the mass consciousness of the planet's inhabitants. The first two layers of simultaneous awareness were present within your psyche, but were blurry and distorted. Examining them in some detail has allowed clarity and understanding adding the third brings forth a realization that you are indeed standing on the first rock of the project's planned diversion. Now it is decision time. Do you participate and continue in sharing a clear picture of the movie in progress all around you? This is a scenario rather than a scene. It is in motion all around you with all three activities interacting on the same stage all within depth, width and height. It goes without saying that the project is the least focused of the activities as yet. That is your job. The basic job description is present within these messages. The framework is there, it is your personal responsibility to "flesh out" the job. The freewill aspect is the ball in your court. Whether you pick it up or walk away is your choice.

Our part to play within this drama, tragedy, or love story (your choice) is to act as the producer of this production. The writing, directing and acting are your contributions. The producer provides the financing and the decisions as to whether the proposed script is something the backers (investors) will approve. If scriptwriters do not bring a proposed scenario to the producers, the producers may decide a certain theme would be saleable and solicit writers to contribute outlines. Since there have been no new paradigm novels, the theatre owner has instructed this producer to solicit new paradigm outlines, beginning with a statement of purpose setting the theme. This is your invitation to participate. Since this is a Cecil B. DeMille type production, collaboration is recommended.

The analogies used are not meant to make light of the situation, but to instill understanding at the subconscious levels of your awareness. Pictures are easily assimilated in clarity. Words are filtered through a myriad of individual past experiences, attitudes, opinions and all the programming each of you carries through the deliberate indoctrination you have received. Movies and television have been their tools of deception. However, the pictures that are brought forth by the imagination are far more powerful. For example, in your not too distant past there was storytelling of myths and legends that invoked the imagination. The current cartoons for children and movies have been provided to repress the inner imagination and stifle the creative instinct. Pictures program the subconscious. Pictures focused with the intent of reprogramming the subconscious accomplish this quickly.

Purposeful intent supported by resolve is focus. The planet and humanity continue to cry out for an end to this scenario, but only humanity can bring the end through the creation of a new plot, a new script and a new play. Freewill allows humanity the choice to continue the present movie or simply have the stage revolve to the next production.

However, there must be a new set (scene) on that stage so that audience participation can be invited to create this play of plays for the planet as a whole.

What more can be done is now out of our hands. The wake up calling is up to each of you as this message comes into your experience. Who is it that you *know* in your heart would resonate with the challenge focused through it? Will you dedicate yourself to this critical cause? Will you read and study the information with the intention of allowing its message to fill the void that resonates within you because of the deceptions of the dark magicians? When you think or speak the small prayer, "I am a human becoming, help me to become", ask for guidance through your feelings that you may know. You are calling forth the vibratory connection to your source, the cause of your life experience here and now. Lines of communication open, and seeming miracles begin to happen through coincidence and synchronicities. Most of all a calm and peaceful attitude becomes prevalent in your experience. Your countenance changes and you <u>know</u> who you are, why you are here and what is to be done in each moment. You have a purpose, a mission and there is hope for this planet after all.

No. 42

In the times that come, those of you who make the choice to become part of the wholistic transformation of this planet and its inhabitants will lead the way through the transformation of yourselves. Mankind is inspired by example not by words, written or spoken. Will you each be as famous as Mother Theresa? No indeed! Your example will be one of living the life of purposeful focus. Each day your intent is to be a human becoming for the purpose of mankind becoming and the planet becoming. This commitment in unison will bring forth an aura of magnetism that will reflect in all aspects of your experience. Will it make you a millionaire? Probably not. Because your focus is to participate in the larger creative flow into an experience that will have parameters that are yet unknown. The basic concept on which all higher dimensions are based is realized in the understanding that the pivot point to upliftment into evolving consciousness is the unified focus of returning to the level of the creator.

The "one-upmanship" of accumulating and maintaining material wealth is a moot point. During the period of chaos facilitating the transition, those with intent to assist in the birthing of the new paradigm, rather than the maintenance of values to be transcended, will be assisted in having available what is needed to superintend facets of organization that are necessary. These will not be in the focus of leadership, but of setting the ideal or archetype of cooperation. Once before, a question was asked for your contemplation. You were asked if you could conceptualize a system in which there were no levels of leadership or hierarchy because they were unnecessary. Unity of focus based on personal responsibility to fulfill the harmonious (shared) goal of "becoming" through individual experience sets up a cooperative environment. Cooperation replaces competition and fear is no longer present. The accumulation of wealth is motivated by the desire for protection which is based in fear of what the future may hold and fed by the empowered ego through competition. "He who dies with the most toys wins" is an apt illustration of this imbalance. "It is easier for a loaded camel to go through the eye of the needle (cultural reference to the small people gate into a town or a house compound) than for a rich man to enter heaven (a state of contentment)." This is true not because of the material things that are accumulated, but because of the basic attitudes that motivate him/her. Retirement funds are necessary because these same attitudes and beliefs bring on disease and degeneration of the body, illustrating the basic lack of trust in the creator's flow that birthed you into this life experience. In a nutshell, the moment you are born, you are taught to begin swimming upstream against the flow of creative expansion. It is now time that you climb out on a rock, take a good look around and then begin swimming within the expansive flow. It is so much easier and "in-joy-able".

Swimming with the flow allows the focus of "becoming" to be thought acting within and upon itself. The resulting harmonious experience is that of being wholly supported in that quest. To accomplish this within an environment of humanity swimming in the opposite direction is impossible unless it is accomplished within a cooperating group that is literally out of that flow. Pulling one's self out of that flow, up on to the rock, carefully perceiving the situation and making the decision to enter the greater flow of the galaxy that is moving within creative expansiveness brings you to a level out of that struggling mass. Once the initial group begins this action by freewill choice, many will join in increasing numbers and a new flow is formed joining the galactic flow. As those of the masses, literally wearing themselves out by spending their creative energy within the struggle, observe your life moving smoothly and easily along within that flow, your mission of reversing the flow will be well under way.

Your return ticket receives its first punch when you pull yourself out and stand on the rock and observe the situation from the level of accepting the situation as reality within the 3rd dimensional realm of Planet Earth. The next punch in your ticket is received when you make your choice/commitment to bring forth a new paradigm of experience. The next is received when you begin the move within your consciousness and change your life expression through thought and action in harmony with your commitment to bring forth this new paradigm of experience with the inhabitants and the planet. You will know the purpose of your incarnation at the fully conscious level and the empty wondering will cease. You then will live in fulfillment of your purpose. To choose otherwise is tearing up your ticket. Can you get a new one? Later maybe, but you will have missed your intended purpose and your intended opportunity.

Reread, contemplate, pray and decide! Freewill is your privilege and your responsibility. Use it in wisdom!

Dear Messengers...

Now that the handbook is complete, it is time that we turn the intention of this flow of information toward the next phase to follow. As the momentum begins to grow, not so much at the actual manifestation level as within the intentions to participate, the idea dawns that a crisis point exists. Our pebble in the pond of the mass consciousness, that no doubt seems ever so tiny to you, is indeed powerful. The shift in perception is the most important beginning point possible. This bypasses the negative emotions of anger and the desire to retaliate. Your bible states "Vengeance is mine, sayeth the Lord." This is a total untruth, but does contain the advice to leave the law of attraction to its natural action. Your misunderstood karmic law, as quoted when there is the desire for someone to get their "just due", is indeed a distorted reference to the law of attraction. When quoting it in judgment it applies in that instance also. "Judge not, lest you be judged." The law of allowance would be wisely used instead as in "I am a human becoming, help me to become." Or "They are humans becoming, help them to become, or he/she is a human becoming, help him/her to become." Indeed this prayer for others is sharing the gift of grace and is allowance indeed! This introduces the next level in the shift in human consciousness, beyond self, to include others through allowance, thereby transcending the need to control.

It is important, when working within the focus intended to be inclusive of the mass consciousness of the entire planet, to forego the desire to quote rules and regulations. These do not sell well, especially with the diversity of understandings within the consciousness of 6 billion beings. Back to the basic of basics in simple language that is easily translatable with as little distortion as possible is most logical. KISS is indeed the rule. Acronyms are interesting shortcuts to recognition. Perhaps we could invent AIAB for attraction, intention, allowance, and balance, or FSTF for the 1st, 2nd, 3rd and 4th. In order to cross language, cultural and religious barriers, simple applications must teach the basic laws without formalities. They must be practically applicable in all life situations and bring forth the desired shift in perspective that translates into changes of attitude and consciousness. It is possible to do this with a few simple words that include AIAB. This seems paradoxical in a world of overwhelming numbers of communications literally moving faster than the speed of light. Of course, overwhelming is the key. The paradox includes the haves who long for greater simplicity and the have nots who long for greater complexity. The inner void remains at all points on the scale of human experience on this planet, except for those who are now aware of the creation of the new paradigm.

It is the first instinct when encountering these messages for individuals to want to rush to "the mission" before study and contemplation bring forth the necessary, fundamental, basic changes in consciousness that allow for synchronistic encounters with people and information to bring into their awareness what their part is. For multitudes, the change in perspective and attitude through the use of the simple prayer is all that is required. These will reap the miracles of a richer life experience, in the midst of chaos, through their focus on the intent within the wave of new consciousness. Spreading the message (word) and applying the basics in their daily lives is the most important mission of all. If applying these is not done at the fundamental levels of human experience, then all the messages are to no avail whatever! These are the ripples. What good are pebbles if the pond remains static? <u>The victim consciousness must be transcended so that humanity can take back its power.</u>

When you share the gift of this information, you must be able to supply feedback to those who receive these messages and reply in a <u>reactive</u> mode. The pent up desire for change is released and direction needs to be given to those who rush to you for guidance. Personal responsibility is another way of saying "take your power and use it with intentional focus to bring balance." The balanced state of experience is necessary to be a functioning part of the ground team. Rereading, studying, contemplating and applying what is within the messages through personal experience will prove the validity of the information and bring forth balance within chaos. The ground team has space for those who are awake, aware, committed, focused and balanced. This brings forth the ability to act rather than react. If it is not yet time for individuals to act, then encourage them to continue to study, share the message and be within the rippling effect while they wait patiently. <u>This is the space you must occupy to be functional and ready. It is putting oil in your lamp so that it may be lit in the moment of opportunity.</u>

So, *become* this consciousness!

The following short list of books will introduce the reader to the awareness that the truth of the deceptions that have been perpetrated on the planetary citizens of Earth is known and has been researched prior to these messages. The ancient records that have been found and more or less accurately translated have revealed much to support the hypothesis briefly mentioned in this book. Chronological information of the activities leading up to the present support the picture of continuing enlargement of the long standing plan for planetary violation. The information in the books listed below should be read with discernment for each author has made their own interpretations, often based on the opinions of others, and come to their own conclusions. These do not necessarily agree with each other or the information within the messages. It is for each to find the confirmations and contradictions within them and to come to their own conclusions. Much more data is available to be found if diligent research is initiated. However, research and reading for verification should not divert those committed to manifesting the New Paradigm of experience from their focus.

Embracing the Rainbow, Vol. II
ISBN: 1-893157-05-9

Becoming, Vol. III
ISBN: 1-893157-07-5

Conspirators' Hierarchy: The Story of the Committee of 300
by John Coleman, ISBN: 0-922356-57-2

Humanity's Extraterrestrial Origins
by Dr. Arthur David Horn, ISBN: 3-931-652-31-9

Gods of Eden
by William Bramley, ISBN: 0-380-71807-3

The Secret of Light
by Walter Russell, ISBN: 1-879605-10-4

The Spiritual Laws and Lessons of the Universe
Lord Michael, St. Germain, Sananda & Druthea,
ISBN: 0-96-40104-6-1

The Thirteenth Tribe
by Arthur Koestler, ISBN: 0-394-40284-7

The Talmud of Immanuel
by Rashid, Meier, Green & Zeigler, ISBN: 0-926524-12-7

Genesis Revisited
By Zecharia Sitchin, ISBN: 0-380-76159-9

The 12th Planet
Book One of "The Earth Chronicles"
By Zecharia Sitchin, ISBN: 0-380-39362-X

To place an order
or to request a catalog
please call 1-800-729-4131
or email:
global@nohoax.com